LOUIS B. WRIGHT, director of the Folger Shakespeare Library, has devoted more than thirty years to the study of the Shakespearean period. In 1926 he completed a doctoral thesis on "Vaudeville Elements in Elizabethan Drama" and subsequently published many articles on the stagecraft and theatre of Shakespeare's day. He is the author of *Middle-Class Culture in Elizabethan England* (1935), *Religion and Empire* (1942), and many other books and essays on the history and literature of the Tudor and Stuart periods. He has taught at the University of North Carolina, the University of California at Los Angeles, Pomona College, the University of Michigan, the University of Minnesota, and other American institutions. From 1932 to 1948 he was instrumental in developing the research program of the Henry E. Huntington Library and Art Gallery. Since 1948 he has been director of the Folger Shakespeare Library in Washington, D.C., which in that time has become one of the leading research institutions of the world for the study of the backgrounds of Anglo-American civilization.

VIRGINIA A. LaMAR is executive secretary of the Folger Shakespeare Library and research assistant to the director. From 1941 to 1946 Miss LaMar was a secretary in the British Admiralty Delegation in Washington, D.C., and in 1945 received the King's Medal for her services. She was coeditor of the *Historie of Travell into Virginia Britania* by William Strachey, published by The Hakluyt Society in 1953.

M. William Shak-speare:

HIS
True Chronicle Historie of the life and
death of King L E A R and his three
Daughters.

With the vnfortunate life of Edgar, sonne
and heire to the Earle of Gloster, and his
sullen and assumed humor of
TOM of Bedlam:

As it was played before the Kings Maiestie at Whit-hall vpon
S. Stephans night in Christmas Hollidayes.

By his Maiesties seruants playing vsually at the Gloabe
on the Bancke-side.

LONDON,
Printed for *Nathaniel Butter*, and are to be sold at his shop in *Pauls*
Church-yard at the signe of the Pide Bull neere
St. Austins Gate. 1608

The Folger Library General Reader's Shakespeare

The Folger Shakespeare Library of Washington, D.C., is a research institution, founded and endowed by Henry Clay Folger and administered by the Trustees of Amherst College. It contains one of the world's most important collections of Shakespeareana. Its materials include extraordinary resources for the study of varied aspects of Western civilization from 1485 to 1715, and are not confined to Shakespeare.

Although the Folger Library's primary purpose is to encourage advanced research in history and literature, it also has a profound concern in stimulating a popular interest in the literature of the Tudor and Stuart periods. This edition of Shakespeare is designed to provide the general reader with a modern text that is clear and understandable, with such notes and explanations as may be needed to clarify obscure words and passages.

GENERAL EDITOR

LOUIS B. WRIGHT

Director, Folger Shakespeare Library

•

ASSISTANT EDITOR

VIRGINIA A. LaMAR

Executive Secretary, Folger Shakespeare Library

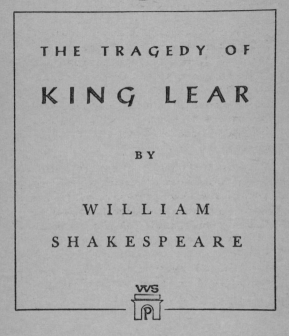

THE TRAGEDY OF
KING LEAR

BY

WILLIAM
SHAKESPEARE

NEW YORK

WASHINGTON SQUARE PRESS, INC.

THE TRAGEDY OF KING LEAR

1960

A new edition of a distinguished literary work now made available in an inexpensive, well-designed format

Published by

L

Washington Square Press, Inc.: Executive Offices, 630 Fifth Avenue;
University Press Division, 32 Washington Place, New York, N.Y.

WASHINGTON SQUARE PRESS editions are distributed in the U.S. by
Affiliated Publishers, Inc., 630 Fifth Avenue, New York 20, N.Y.

Preface

This edition of *King Lear* is designed to make available a readable text of one of Shakespeare's greatest plays. In the centuries since Shakespeare lived, many changes have occurred in the meanings of words, and some clarification of Shakespeare's vocabulary may be helpful. To provide the reader with necessary notes in the most accessible format, we have placed them on the pages facing the text that they explain. We have tried to make these notes as brief and simple as possible. Preliminary to the text we have also included a brief statement of essential information about Shakespeare and his stage. Readers desiring more detailed information should refer to the books suggested in the references, and if still further information is needed, the bibliographies in those books will provide the necessary clues to the literature of the subject.

L. B. W.
V. A. L.

December 10, 1956

The Droeshout engraving of William Shakespeare.
From the title page of the First Folio

The Author

WHEN WILLIAM SHAKESPEARE wrote *The Tragedy of King Lear* in 1605 or early in 1606, he was already one of the most popular dramatists of his day, as well as an actor and a producer. Most of his best comedies, his great history plays, and some of his finest tragedies were behind him. Only *Macbeth, Antony and Cleopatra, Coriolanus, Timon of Athens, Pericles, Cymbeline, Winter's Tale, The Tempest,* and *Henry VIII* were yet to be written. With *King Lear* Shakespeare reached a peak of dramatic expression in a play that ranks with the drama of Sophocles and Euripides as one of the supreme examples of tragedy.

Eight years before *King Lear* was produced, Shakespeare was so well known as a literary and dramatic craftsman that Francis Meres, a young preacher, in a volume called *Palladis Tamia: Wits Treasury* (1598), referred in flattering terms to him as "mellifluous and honey-tongued Shakespeare," famous for his *Venus and Adonis,* his *Lucrece,* and "his sugared sonnets" which were circulating "among his private friends." Meres observes further that "as Plautus and Seneca are accounted the best for comedy and tragedy among the Latins, so Shakespeare among the English is the most excellent in both kinds for the stage" and he mentions a dozen plays that had made a name for Shakespeare. He concludes with the remark "that the Muses would speak with Shakespeare's fine filed phrase if they would speak English."

To those acquainted with the history of the Elizabethan and Jacobean periods, it is incredible that anyone should be so naïve or ignorant as to doubt the reality of Shakespeare as the author of the plays that bear his name. Yet so much nonsense has been written about other "candidates" for the plays that it is well to remind readers that no credible evidence that would stand up in a court of law has ever been adduced to prove either that Shakespeare did not write his plays or that anybody else wrote them. All the theories offered for the authorship of Francis Bacon, the Earl of Derby, the Earl of Oxford, the Earl of Hertford, Christopher Marlowe, and a score of other candidates are mere conjectures spun from the active imaginations of persons who confuse hypothesis and conjecture with evidence.

As Meres' statement of 1598 indicates, Shakespeare was already a popular playwright whose name carried weight at the box office. The obvious reputation of Shakespeare as early as 1598 makes the effort to prove him a myth one of the most absurd in the history of human perversity.

The anti-Shakespeareans talk darkly about a plot of vested interests to maintain the authorship of Shakespeare. Nobody has any vested interest in Shakespeare, but every scholar is interested in the truth and in the quality of evidence advanced by special pleaders who set forth hypotheses in place of facts.

The anti-Shakespeareans base their arguments upon a few simple premises, all of them false. These false premises are that Shakespeare was an unlettered yokel without any schooling, that nothing is known about Shakespeare, and that only a noble lord or the equivalent in background could have written the plays. The facts are that more is known about Shakespeare than about most dramatists of his day, that he had a very good education acquired in the Stratford Grammar School, that the plays show no evidence of profound book learning, and that the knowledge of kings and courts evident in the plays is no greater than any intelligent young man could have picked up at second hand. Most anti-Shakespeareans are naïve and betray an obvious snobbery. The author of their favorite plays, they imply, must have had a college diploma framed and hung on his study wall like the one in their dentist's office, and obviously so great a writer must have had a title or some equally significant evidence of exalted social background. They forget that genius has a way of cropping up in unexpected places and that none of the great creative writers of the world got his inspiration in a college or university course.

William Shakespeare was the son of John Shakespeare of Stratford-upon-Avon, a substantial citizen of that small but busy market town in the center of the rich agricultural county of Warwick. John Shakespeare kept a shop, what we would call a general store; he dealt in wool and other produce and gradually acquired property. As a youth, John Shakespeare had learned the trade of glover and leather worker. There is no contemporary evidence that the elder Shakespeare was a butcher, though the anti-Shakespeareans like to talk about the ignorant "butcher's boy of Stratford." Their only evidence is a statement by gossipy John Aubrey, more than a century after William Shakespeare's birth, that young William followed his father's trade and when he killed a calf "he would do it in a high style and make a speech." We would like to believe the story true, but Aubrey is not a very credible witness.

John Shakespeare probably continued to operate a farm at Snitterfield that his father had leased. He married Mary Arden, daughter of his father's landlord, a man of some property. The third of their eight children was William, baptized on April 26, 1564, and probably born three days before. At least it is conventional to celebrate April 23 as his birthday.

The Stratford records give considerable information about John Shakespeare. We know that he held several municipal offices including those of alderman and mayor. In 1580 he was in some sort of legal difficulty and was fined for neglecting a summons of the Court of Queen's Bench requiring him to appear at Westminster and be bound over to keep the peace.

As a citizen and alderman of Stratford, John Shakespeare was entitled to send his son to the grammar school free. Though the records are lost, there can be no reason to doubt that this is where young William received his education. As any student of the period knows, the grammar schools provided the basic education in Latin learning and literature. The Elizabethan grammar school is not to be confused with modern grammar schools. Many cultivated men of the day received all their formal education in the grammar schools. At the universities in this period a student would have received little training that would have inspired him to be a creative writer. At Stratford young Shakespeare would have acquired a familiarity with Latin and some little knowledge of Greek. He would have read Latin authors and become acquainted with the plays of Plautus and Terence. Undoubtedly in this period of his life he received that stimulation to read and explore for himself the world of ancient and modern history which he later utilized in his plays. The youngster who does not acquire this type of intellectual curiosity *before* college days rarely develops the kind of mind Shakespeare demonstrated as a result of a college course. His learning in books was anything but profound, but he clearly had the probing curiosity that sent him in search of information, and he had a keenness in the observation of nature and of humankind that finds reflection in his poetry.

There is little documentation for Shakespeare's boyhood. There is little reason why there should be. Nobody knew that he was going to be a dramatist about whom any scrap of information would be prized in the centuries to come. He was merely an active and vigorous youth of Stratford, perhaps assisting his father in his business, and no Boswell bothered to write down facts about him. The most important record that we have is a marriage license issued by the Bishop of Worcester on November 28, 1582, to permit William Shakespeare to marry Anne Hathaway, seven or eight years his senior; furthermore, the Bishop permitted the marriage after reading the banns only once instead of three times, evidence of the desire for haste. The need was explained on May 26, 1583, when the christening of Susanna, daughter of William and Anne Shakespeare, was recorded at Stratford. Two years later, on February 2, 1585, the records show the birth of twins to the Shakespeares, a boy and a girl who were christened Hamnet and Judith.

Presumption:

An Elizabethan gallant.
From the Trevelyon MS. in the Folger Shakespeare Library

Presumptious. Woman

A fashionable lady of the Elizabethan period.
From the Trevelyon MS. in the Folger Shakespeare Library

What William Shakespeare was doing in Stratford during the early years of his married life, or when he went to London, we do not know. It has been conjectured that he tried his hand at school teaching, but that is a mere guess. There is a legend that he left Stratford to escape a charge of poaching in the park of Sir Thomas Lucy at Charlecote, but there is no proof of this. There is also a legend that when first he came to London he earned his living by holding horses outside a playhouse and presently was given employment inside, but there is nothing better than eighteenth-century hearsay for this. How Shakespeare broke into the London theatres as dramatist and actor, we do not know. But lack of information is not surprising, for Elizabethans did not write their autobiographies, and we know even less about the lives of many writers and some men of affairs than we know about Shakespeare. By 1592 he was so well established and popular that he incurred the envy of the dramatist and pamphleteer, Robert Greene, who referred to him as an "upstart crow . . . in his own conceit the only Shakescene in a country." From this time onward contemporary allusions and references in legal documents enable the scholar to chart Shakespeare's career with greater accuracy than is possible with most other Elizabethan dramatists.

By 1594 Shakespeare was a member of the company of actors known then as the Lord Chamberlain's Men. After the accession of James I in 1603, the company would have the sovereign for their patron and would be known as the King's Men. During the period of its greatest prosperity this company would have as its principal theatres the Globe and the Blackfriars. Shakespeare was both an actor and a shareholder in the

Queen Elizabeth in 1585.
Engraved from a portrait by Nicholas Hilliard

company. He thus had three sources of income: from the sale of his plays to the company, from his wages as an actor, and from his share of the profits of the theatrical company. Tradition has assigned him such acting roles as Adam in *As You Like It* and the Ghost in *Hamlet*, a modest place on the stage that suggests that he may have had other duties in the management of the company. Such conclusions, however, are based on surmise.

What we do know is that his plays were popular and that he was highly successful in his triple vocation. His first play may have been *The Comedy of Errors*, acted perhaps in 1591. Certainly this was one of his earliest plays. The three parts of *Henry VI* were acted sometime between 1590 and 1592. Critics are not in agreement about precisely how much Shakespeare wrote of these three plays. *Richard III* probably dates from 1593. With this play Shakespeare captured the imagination of Elizabethan audiences, then enormously interested in historical plays. With *Richard III*, Shakespeare also gave an interpretation pleasing to the Tudors of the rise to power of the grandfather of Queen Elizabeth. From this time onward, Shakespeare's plays followed on the stage in rapid succession: *Titus Andronicus, The Taming of the Shrew, The Two Gentlemen of Verona, Love's Labour's Lost, Romeo and Juliet, Richard II, A Midsummer Night's Dream, King John, The Merchant of Venice, Henry IV*, Pts. I and II, *Much Ado About Nothing, Henry V, Julius Caesar, As You Like It, Twelfth Night, Hamlet, The Merry Wives of Windsor, All's Well That Ends Well, Measure for Measure, Othello, King Lear*, and nine others that followed before Shakespeare retired completely, about 1613.

In the course of his career in London, he made enough money to enable him to retire to Stratford with a competence. His purchase on May 4, 1597, of New Place, then next to the largest dwelling in Stratford, a "pretty house of brick and timber," with a handsome garden, indicates his increasing prosperity. There his wife and children lived while he busied himself in the London theatres. The summer before he acquired New Place his life was darkened by the death of his only son, Hamnet, a child of eleven. In May 1602, Shakespeare purchased one hundred and seven acres of fertile farmland near Stratford and a few months later bought a cottage and garden across the alley from New Place. About 1611, he seems to have returned permanently to Stratford, for the next year a legal document refers to him as "William Shakespeare of Stratford-upon-Avon . . . gentleman." To achieve the desired appellation of gentleman, William Shakespeare had seen to it that the College of Heralds in 1596 granted his father a coat of arms. In one step he thus became a second-generation gentleman.

Shakespeare's daughter, Susanna, made a good match in 1607 with Dr. John Hall, a prominent and prosperous Stratford physician. His second daughter, Judith, did not marry until she was thirty-two years old, and then, under somewhat scandalous circumstances, she married Thomas Quiney, a Stratford vintner. On March 25, 1616, Shakespeare made his will, bequeathing his landed property to Susanna, £300 to Judith, certain sums to other relatives, and his second-best bed to his wife Anne. Much has been made of the second-best bed, but the legacy probably indicates only that Anne liked that particular bed. Shakespeare, following the practice of the time, may have already arranged with Susanna for his wife's care. Finally, on April 23, 1616, the anniversary of his birth, William Shakespeare died, and he was buried on April 25 within the chancel of Trinity Church as befitted an honored citizen. On August 6, 1623, a few months before the publication of the collected edition of Shakespeare's plays, Anne Shakespeare joined her husband in death.

THE PUBLICATION OF HIS PLAYS

DURING his lifetime Shakespeare made no effort to publish any of his plays, though eighteen appeared in print in single-play editions known as quartos. Some of these are corrupt versions known as "bad quartos." No quarto, so far as is known, had the author's approval. Plays were not considered "literature" any more than radio and television scripts today are considered literature. Dramatists sold their plays outright to the theatrical companies and it was usually considered in the company's interest to keep plays from getting into print. To achieve a reputation as a man of letters Shakespeare wrote his *Sonnets,* and his narrative poems, *Venus and Adonis* and *The Rape of Lucrece,* but he probably never dreamed that his plays would establish his reputation as a literary genius. Only Ben Jonson, a man known for his colossal conceit, had the crust to call his plays *Works,* as he did when he published an edition in 1616. But men laughed at Ben Jonson.

After Shakespeare's death, two of his old colleagues in the King's Men, John Heming and Henry Condell, decided that it would be a good thing to print, in more accurate versions than were then available, the plays already published and eighteen additional plays not previously published in quarto. In 1623 appeared *Mr. William Shakespeare's Comedies, Histories, & Tragedies. Published according to the True Originall Copies. London. Printed by Isaac Iaggard, and Ed. Blount.* This was the famous First Folio, a work that had the authority of Shakespeare's associates. The only play commonly attributed to Shakespeare that was omitted in the First Folio was *Pericles.* In their preface "To the great Variety of Readers," Heming and Condell state that whereas "you were abused with diverse stolen and surreptitious copies, maimed and deformed by the frauds and stealths of injurious impostors that exposed them, even those are now offered to your view cured and perfect of their limbs; and all the rest, absolute in their numbers, as he conceived them." What they used for printer's copy is one of the vexed problems of scholarship, and skilled bibliographers have devoted years of study to the question of the relation of the "copy" for the First Folio to Shakespeare's manuscripts. In some cases it is clear that the editors corrected printed quarto versions of the plays, probably by comparison with playhouse scripts. Whether these scripts were in Shakespeare's autograph is anybody's guess. No manuscript of any play in Shakespeare's handwriting has survived. Indeed, very few play manuscripts from this period by any author are extant. The Tudor and Stuart periods had not yet learned to prize autographs and authors' original manuscripts.

Since the First Folio contains eighteen plays not previously printed, it is the only source for these. For the other eighteen, which had appeared in quarto versions, the First Folio also has the authority of an edition prepared and overseen by Shakespeare's colleagues and professional associates. But since editorial standards in 1623 were far from strict, and Heming and Condell were actors rather than editors by profession, the texts are sometimes careless. The printing and proofreading of the First Folio also left much to be desired, and some garbled passages have to be corrected and emended. The "good" quarto texts have to be taken into account in preparing a modern edition.

Because of the great popularity of Shakespeare through the centuries, the First Folio has become a prized book but it is not a very rare one, for it is estimated that 238 copies are extant. The Folger Shakespeare Library in Washington, D.C., has seventy-nine copies of the First Folio, collected by the founder, Henry Clay Folger, who believed that a collation of as many texts as possible would reveal significant facts about the text of Shakespeare's plays. Dr. Charlton Hinman, using an ingenious machine of his own invention for mechanical collating, has made many discoveries that throw light on Shakespeare's text and on printing practices of the day.

The probability is that the First Folio of 1623 had an edition of between 1,000 and 1,250 copies. It is believed that it sold for £1, which made it an expensive book, for £1 in 1623 was equivalent to something between $40 and $50 in modern purchasing power.

During the seventeenth century, Shakespeare was sufficiently popular to warrant three later editions in folio size, the Second Folio of 1632, the Third Folio of 1663-64, and the Fourth Folio of 1685. The Third

Folio added six other plays ascribed to Shakespeare but these are apocryphal.

THE SHAKESPEAREAN THEATRE

THE THEATRES in which Shakespeare's plays were performed were vastly different from those we know today. The stage was a platform that jutted out into the area now occupied by the first rows of seats on the main floor, what is called the "orchestra" in America and the "pit" in England. This platform had no curtain to come down at the ends of acts and scenes. And although simple stage properties were available, the Elizabethan theatre lacked both the machinery and the elaborate moveable scenery of the modern theatre. In the rear of the platform stage was a curtained area that could be used as an inner room, a tomb, or any such scene that might be required. A balcony above this inner room, and perhaps balconies on the sides of the stage, could represent the upper deck of a ship, the entry to Juliet's room, or a prison window. A trap door in the stage provided an entrance for ghosts and devils from the nether regions, and a similar trap in the canopied structure over the stage, known as the "heavens," made it possible to let down angels on a rope. These primitive stage arrangements help to account for many elements in Elizabethan plays. For example, since there was no curtain, the dramatist had to write into his play action to clear the stage at the ends of acts and scenes. The funeral march at the end of *Hamlet* is not there merely for atmosphere; Shakespeare had to get the corpses off the stage.

Before London had buildings designed exclusively

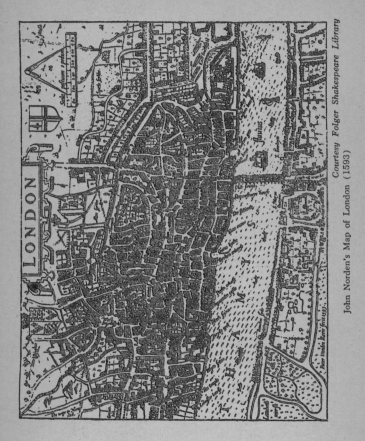

John Norden's Map of London (1593)

The Swan (39), the Bear Garden (38), and the Globe (37).
From Merian's View of London (1638)

for theatrical entertainment, plays were given in inns and taverns. The characteristic inn of the period had an inner courtyard with rooms opening onto balconies overlooking the yard. Players could set up their temporary stages at one end of the yard and audiences could find seats on the balconies out of the weather. The poorer sort could stand or sit on the cobblestones in the yard, which was open to the sky. The first theatres followed this construction, and throughout the Elizabethan period the large public theatres had a yard in front of the stage open to the weather, with two or three tiers of covered balconies extending around the theatre. This physical structure again influenced the writing of plays. Because a dramatist wanted the actors to be heard, he frequently wrote into his play orations that could be delivered with declamatory effect. He also provided spectacle, buffoonery, and broad jests to keep the riotous groundlings in the yard entertained and quiet.

In another respect the Elizabethan theatre differed greatly from ours. It had no actresses. All women's roles were taken by boys, sometimes recruited from the boys' choirs of the London churches. Some of these youths acted their roles with great skill and the Elizabethans did not seem to be aware of any incongruity. The first actresses on the professional English stage appeared after the Restoration of Charles II in 1660 when exiled Englishmen brought back from France practices of the French stage.

London in the Elizabethan period, as now, was the center of theatrical interest, though wandering actors from time to time traveled through the country performing in inns, halls, and the houses of the nobility. The first professional playhouse, called simply The

Theatre, was erected by James Burbage, father of Shakespeare's colleague Richard Burbage, in 1576 on lands of the old Holywell Priory adjacent to Finsbury Fields, a playground and park area just north of the city walls. It had the advantage of being outside the city's jurisdiction and yet was near enough to be easily accessible. Soon after The Theatre was opened, another playhouse called The Curtain was erected in the same neighborhood. Both of these playhouses had open courtyards and were probably polygonal in shape.

About the time The Curtain opened, Richard Farrant, Master of the Chapel Royal at Windsor and of St. Paul's, conceived the idea of opening a "private" theatre in the old monastery buildings of the Blackfriars, not far from St. Paul's Cathedral in the heart of the city. This theatre was ostensibly to train the choir boys in plays for presentation at Court. Actually, Farrant managed to present plays to paying audiences and achieved considerable success until aristocratic neighbors complained and had the theatre closed. This first Blackfriars Theatre was significant, however, because it popularized the boy actors in a professional way and it paved the way for a second theatre in the Blackfriars which Shakespeare's company took over more than thirty years later. By the last years of the sixteenth century, London had at least six professional theatres and still others were erected during the reign of James I.

The Globe Theatre, the playhouse that most people connect with Shakespeare, was erected early in 1599 on the Bankside, the area across the Thames from the city. Its construction had a dramatic beginning, for on the night of December 28, 1598, James Burbage's sons, Cuthbert and Richard, gathered together a crew who

London Bridge.
From Visscher's View of London (1616)

tore down the old Theatre in Holywell and carted the timbers across the river to a site that they had chosen for a new playhouse. The reason for this clandestine operation was a row with the landowner over the lease to the Holywell property. The site chosen for the Globe was another playground outside of the city's jurisdiction, a region of somewhat unsavory character. Not far away was the Bear Garden, an amphitheatre devoted to the baiting of bears and bulls. This was also the region occupied by many houses of ill fame licensed by the Bishop of Winchester and the source of a substantial revenue to him. But it was easily accessible either from London Bridge or by means of the cheap boats operated by the London watermen, and it had the great advantage of being beyond the authority of the Puritanical aldermen of London, who frowned on plays because they lured apprentices from work, filled their heads with improper ideas, and generally exerted a bad influence. The aldermen also complained that the crowds drawn together in the theatre helped to spread the plague.

The Globe was the handsomest theatre up to its time. It was a large octagonal building, open like its predecessors to the sky in the center, but capable of seating a large audience in its covered balconies. To erect and operate the Globe, the Burbages organized a syndicate composed of the leading members of the dramatic company, of which Shakespeare was a member. Since it was open to the weather, and depended on natural light, plays had to be given in the afternoon. This caused no hardship in the long afternoons of an English summer, but in the winter, the weather was a great handicap and discouraged all except the hardiest.

For that reason, in 1608 Shakespeare's company was glad to take over the lease of the second Blackfriars Theatre, a substantial, roomy hall reconstructed within the fabric of the old monastery building. This theatre was protected from the weather and its stage was artificially lighted by chandeliers of candles. This became the winter playhouse for Shakespeare's company and at once proved so popular that the congestion of traffic created an embarrassing problem. Stringent regulations had to be made for the movement of coaches in the vicinity. Shakespeare's company continued to use the Globe during the summer months. In 1613 a squib fired from a cannon during a performance of *Henry VIII* fell on the thatched roof and the Globe burned to the ground. The next year it was rebuilt.

London had other famous theatres. The Rose, just west of the Globe, was built by Philip Henslowe, a semi-literate denizen of the Bankside, who became one of the most important theatrical owners and producers of the Tudor and Stuart period. What is more important for historians, he kept a detailed account book, which provides much of our information about theatrical history in his period. Another famous theatre on the Bankside was the Swan, which a Dutch priest, Johannes de Witt, visited in 1596. The crude drawing of the stage which he made was copied by his friend Arend Van Buchell; it is one of the important pieces of contemporary evidence for theatrical construction. De Witt described the Swan as capable of holding three thousand spectators. Among the other theatres, the Fortune, north of the city, on Golding Lane, and the Red Bull, even farther away from the city, off St. John's Street, were the most popular. The Red Bull, much fre-

tectum

porticus

sedilia

orchestra

ingressus

mimorum
aedes

proscænium

planities siue arena

hunc sed. pistori et parui turres, bestiarum concitat-
oni destinatum, in quo multi ursi tauri, et stupenda
magnitudinis canes, distinctis caucis et septis alluntur, qui ad

Interior of the Swan Theatre (1596).
From a drawing by Johannes de Witt

quented by apprentices, favored sensational and sometimes rowdy plays.

The actors who kept all of these theatres going were
organized into companies under the protection of some
noble patron. Traditionally actors had enjoyed a low
reputation. In some of the ordinances they were classed
as vagrants; in the phraseology of the time, "rogues,
vagabonds, sturdy beggars, and common players" were
all listed together as undesirables. To escape penalties
often meted out to these characters, organized groups of
actors managed to gain the protection of various per-
sonages of high degree. In the later years of Elizabeth's reign, a group flourished under the name of the
Queen's Men; another group had the protection of the
Lord Admiral and were known as the Lord Admiral's
Men. Edward Alleyn, son-in-law of Philip Henslowe,
was the leading spirit in the Lord Admiral's Men. Besides the adult companies, troupes of boy actors from
time to time also enjoyed considerable popularity.
Among these were the Children of Paul's and the Children of the Chapel Royal.

The company with which Shakespeare had a long
association had for its patron Henry Carey, Lord Huns-
don, the Lord Chamberlain, and hence they were
known as the Lord Chamberlain's Men. After the accession of James I they became the King's Men. This company was the great rival of the Lord Admiral's Men,
managed by Henslowe and Alleyn.

All was not easy for the players in Shakespeare's time,
for the aldermen of London were always eager for an
excuse to close up the Blackfriars and any other theatres
in their jurisdiction. The theatres outside the jurisdiction of London were not immune from interference, for

they might be shut up by order of the Privy Council for meddling in politics or for various other offenses, or they might be closed in time of plague lest they spread infection. During plague times the actors usually went on tour and played the provinces wherever they could find an audience. Particularly frightening were the plagues of 1592-1594 and 1613 when the theatres closed and the players, like many other Londoners, had to take to the country.

Though players had a low social status, they enjoyed great popularity and one of the favorite forms of entertainment at Court was the performance of plays. To be commanded to perform at Court conferred great prestige upon a company of players, and printers when they published plays frequently noted that fact. Many of Shakespeare's plays were performed before the sovereign and Shakespeare himself undoubtedly acted in some of these plays.

THE HISTORY OF *King Lear*

SHAKESPEARE's tragedy of *King Lear* was performed before King James I as part of the Christmas celebration in 1606. The title page of the quarto version printed in 1608 boasts that it is now published "As it was played before the King's Majesty at Whitehall upon St. Stephen's night in Christmas Holidays. By his Majesty's servants playing usually at the Globe on the Bankside." Precisely when it was written is not known, but it was probably composed during the year 1606 or late 1605. It is supposed that Shakespeare may be referring to eclipses that occurred in September and October 1605 in the allusion to "these late eclipses in the sun and moon."

The story of King Lear, one of the mythical kings who reigned in the dim and undated past, was well known in British legend. In Raphael Holinshed's *Chronicles* the date of Lear's reign is given as "the year of the world 3105." Whether there was actually a British king of this name nobody knows. But he was sufficiently real in folklore to arouse interest during a period when works concerning British antiquities were making a wide appeal to Englishmen of all classes. The tale of the impetuous old king had been familiar for centuries. Appearing first in Geoffrey of Monmouth's chronicle, *Historia Britonum,* composed about 1135, it was quickly assimilated into the legendary history of Britain and found its way into chronicles and other literary works read by the Elizabethans. Versions of the tale in the 1574 edition of *Mirror for Magistrates,* in Holinshed's *Chronicles,* and in Edmund Spenser's *Faerie Queene* may have furnished Shakespeare with elements of his plot. The subplot dealing with the troubles of Gloucester he took from a story in Philip Sidney's *Arcadia.* Furthermore, an older play called *The True Chronicle History of King Leir* (*sic*), acted in the early 1590's and printed in 1605, may have suggested to Shakespeare the idea of a new play on a subject already well known and popular.

How well Shakespeare's play was received when it was acted for the general public, we do not know, but in some version it has remained alive as an active stage play from that day to this.

During the later seventeenth century, an adaptation of Shakespeare's *King Lear* by Nahum Tate, one of the popular dramatists of the Restoration period, superseded the original play. Published in 1681, the Tate adaptation provided elements that persisted until well into the nineteenth century. As modern screen versions of tragedies sometimes soften the harsh endings of classic plays, so Tate gave *King Lear* a happy ending in which virtue was rewarded and all was made right. To sweeten the tragedy still further, Tate contrived a love affair between Edgar and Cordelia. " 'Twas my good fortune," Tate explains, "to light on one expedient to rectify what was wanting in the regularity and probability of the tale, which was to run through the whole a love betwixt Edgar and Cordelia that never changed word with each other in the original. This renders Cordelia's indifference and her father's passion in the first scene probable. It likewise gives countenance to Edgar's disguise, making that a generous design that was before a poor shift to save his life." Mawkish and sentimental as Tate's adaptation was, it met with favor. David Garrick in the mid-eighteenth century continued to accept some of Tate's "improvements" and retained the happy ending. Finally, in 1838, William Charles Macready restored Shakespeare's text to the acting stage.

THE QUALITY OF THE PLAY

King Lear is one of Shakespeare's greatest plays, a tragedy of profound insight, cosmic in the universality of its appeal. To the reader, or the spectator of the stage performance, the play is not merely the tale of a king of ancient Britain but instead it is a story that deals with the eternal theme of the relations of parents and children. "How sharper than a serpent's tooth it is / To have a thankless child" has been echoed by thousands of parents who have experienced the misery of a child's ingratitude. The reader forgets that Lear is a king of Britain. He is a rash, impetuous, and spoiled old man who by his own folly brings down upon his head punishments that chasten and transform him. His daughters are the instruments of Fate in the re-education of a man who had reached old age without achieving the wisdom—and the humility—that maturity and experience should bring. Only incidentally is Lear king of Britain. In the reader's mind he might just as easily be the headstrong old man next door.

The theme of the play may be described as the education and purification of Lear. Beginning with Act I, the play rapidly discloses the steps in Lear's transformation. When we first see him he is proud, dictatorial, unreasoning, and unreasonable. Piqued in his vanity by Cordelia, he summarily disinherits her and delivers himself into the power of the rapacious Regan and Goneril. The consequences of his folly soon overtake him, and Lear realizes his mistakes. But the purging of his soul of vanity, impulsiveness, and rage requires the humiliations meted out by his cruel daughters, the terrors of the storm on the barren heath, and the final revelation of the loyalty of Kent and Cordelia. By the time Lear is cured of his follies nothing is left of life, but he has at last come to the realization of the futility of those vanities of the world that had once seemed so important. In prison he and Cordelia will

> . . . . hear poor rogues
> Talk of court news; and we'll talk with them too,

Who loses and who wins; who's in, who's out;
And take upon's the mystery of things,
As if we were God's spies; and we'll wear out,
In a walled prison, packs and sects of great ones
That ebb and flow by the moon.

High place and position are no longer matters of any concern. In the pelting storm, pride of position meant nothing, and though he might have been "every inch a king," he learned that he was "not ague-proof." As Lear in his madness tore off his clothes, so he discarded the trappings of his former life and his former beliefs.

The subplot relating the sufferings of old Gloucester at the hands of his vengeful and grasping bastard son Edmund parallels the main plot and helps to intensify the emotional impact of Lear's story. With more care than is usual in the structure of an Elizabethan play, Shakespeare wove the incidents of the subplot into the main action in such a way as to heighten the emphasis rather than distract from his theme.

The Fool, who serves as a sort of chorus or commentary, is also there to emphasize the tragedy of Lear and to reflect at times the vague thoughts flitting through the old king's mind. He was so little understood in the late seventeenth and eighteenth centuries that he was omitted, but Shakespeare did not include him merely because the Fool was a convention of Elizabethan drama. His presence affords some of the most subtle and moving passages in the play.

In its philosophic implications, *King Lear* is pagan and pessimistic. There is no comfortable belief in the best of all possible worlds in this play. Man is in the hands of Fate, an arbitrary Fate that turns the wheel of Fortune mechanically. "As flies to wanton boys, are we to the gods; / They kill us for their sport" is the comment of Gloucester who voices the pagan doctrine of the play. Some biographers have seen in *King Lear* a reflection of a personal tragedy in Shakespeare's life, but we have no proof for such a belief. *King Lear* may simply reflect the fatalistic and stoical attitudes that characterized much of the writing of the Jacobean period. "Men must endure / Their going hence, even as their coming hither: / Ripeness is all," Edgar observes in one of the passages that indicate the stoical acceptance of the decisions of Fate. It was a belief that shifting fortunes and the rise and fall of reputations had forced upon many men in this age. From Shakespeare's day to our own, men and women have contemplated the blind and inexplicable turns of fortune and have echoed the pessimism implicit in *King Lear*.

THE TEXT

THE EDITORS of the present edition of *King Lear* have taken the version in the First Folio as the basis of their text, but as editors have generally done, they have collated it with the First Quarto and have adopted the readings of the Quarto text in passages where they seemed better. Spelling has been modernized and punctuation has been altered to give the sense that was intended.

The editors of the First Folio apparently used a corrected text of the First Quarto as printer's copy but they omitted approximately 300 lines from the Quarto text and added approximately 100 lines not found in the Quarto. As is the practice of modern editors, we have restored these omitted lines.

Neither the Folio nor the Quarto text contains settings for the various scenes, and stage directions are few and inadequate. Accordingly, settings and stage directions have been added to illuminate the action. These and additions to directions adopted from the original texts are enclosed in square brackets.

The numbering of lines is literally line by line and therefore does not agree with the lineation in most concordances, which follow the convention of counting two consecutive half-lines of verse as one metrical line.

References for Further Reading

MANY READERS will want suggestions for further reading about Shakespeare and his times. The literature in this field is enormous but a few references will serve as guides to further study. A simple and useful little book is Gerald Sanders, *A Shakespeare Primer* (New York, 1950). More detailed but still not too voluminous to be confusing is Hazelton Spencer, *The Art and Life of William Shakespeare* (New York, 1940), which, like Sanders' handbook, contains a brief annotated list of useful books on various aspects of the subject. The most detailed and scholarly work providing complete factual information about Shakespeare is Sir Edmund Chambers, *William Shakespeare: A Study of Facts and Problems* (2 vols., Oxford, 1930). For detailed, factual information about the Elizabethan and seventeenth-century stages, the definitive reference works are Sir Edmund Chambers, *The Elizabethan Stage* (4 vols., Oxford, 1923) and Gerald E. Bentley, *The Jacobean and Caroline Stage* (5 vols., Oxford, 1941-56).

Although specialists disagree about details of stage construction, the reader will find essential information in John C. Adams, *The Globe Playhouse: Its Design and Equipment* (Cambridge, Mass., 1942). A model of the Globe playhouse made by Dr. Adams is on permanent exhibition in the Folger Shakespeare Library in Washington, D. C. An easily read history of the early theatres is J. Q. Adams, *Shakespearean Playhouses: A History of English Theatres from the Beginnings to the Restoration* (Boston, 1917).

A brief, clear, and accurate account of Tudor history is S. T. Bindoff, *The Tudors* in the Penguin series. A readable general history is G. M. Trevelyan, *The History of England*, first published in 1926 and available in many editions since. Trevelyan's *English Social History*, first published in 1942 and also available in many editions, provides fascinating information about England in all periods. Sir John Neale, *Queen Elizabeth* (London, 1934) is the best study of the great Queen. Various aspects of literature and society are treated in Louis B. Wright, *Middle-Class Culture in Elizabethan England* (Chapel Hill, N. C., 1935).

[*Dramatis Personae.*

Lear, King of Britain.
King of France.
Duke of Burgundy.
Duke of Cornwall, Regan's husband.
Duke of Albany, Goneril's husband.
Earl of Kent.
Earl of Gloucester.
Edgar, Gloucester's son.
Edmund, Gloucester's bastard son.
Curan, a courtier.
Old Man, *Gloucester's* tenant.
Doctor.
The Fool.
Oswald, Goneril's steward.
A Captain in *Edmund's* employ.
Gentlemen.
A Herald.
Servants of *Cornwall.*

Goneril,
Regan, } *Lear's* daughters.
Cordelia,

Knights in *Lear's* service, Officers,
　　　Messengers, Soldiers, Attendants.

SCENE.—*Britain*]

KING LEAR

ACT I

I. i. The opening scene immediately reveals the situation about which the whole play revolves. Lear, rash and hasty, has planned to rid himself of worries by dividing his kingdom among his three daughters, Regan, Goneril, and Cordelia. Before making the division he asks each to attest her love for him. Disgusted at the fulsome but hollow pretensions of her two older sisters, Cordelia refuses to flatter her father, and is disinherited. When his old courtier the Earl of Kent protests, Lear banishes him. The King of France recognizes Cordelia's sincerity and accepts her as his betrothed after the Duke of Burgundy has refused to take a penniless bride. The scene concludes with Regan and Goneril already planning to curb the activities of the king, whom they consider senile.

||||||||||||||||||||||||||||||||||||||

1. **more affected:** favored
5-6. **curiosity:** painstaking examination
6. **moiety:** share
10. **brazed:** brazened
11. **conceive:** understand

ACT I

Scene I. [Inside Lear's Palace.]

Enter Kent, Gloucester, and Edmund [in rear].

Kent. I thought the King had more affected the Duke
of Albany than Cornwall.

Glou. It did always seem so to us; but now, in the division of the kingdom, it appears not which of the Dukes
he values most, for qualities are so weighed that curi-   5
osity in neither can make choice of either's moiety.

Kent. Is not this your son, my lord?

Glou. His breeding, sir, hath been at my charge. I
have so often blushed to acknowledge him that now I
am brazed to it.   10

Kent. I cannot conceive you.

Glou. Sir, this young fellow's mother could, where-
upon she grew round-wombed, and had indeed, sir, a
son for her cradle ere she had a husband for her bed. Do
you smell a fault?   15

Kent. I cannot wish the fault undone, the issue of it
being so proper.

Glou. But I have a son, sir, by order of law, some year
elder than this, who yet is no dearer in my account. Though
this knave came something saucily to the world before   20

I

22. **whoreson:** bastard

28. **sue:** make an effort

29. **study deserving:** try to be worthy

30. **He hath been out nine years:** presumably Edmund has been out of the country, perhaps on military service.

Stage Dir., **sennet:** the sounding of trumpets to announce the arrival of a person or company of importance

43. **constant will:** firm intention

he was sent for, yet was his mother fair, there was good
sport at his making, and the whoreson must be acknowl-
edged.—Do you know this noble gentleman, Edmund?

Edm. [*Advancing*] No, my lord.

Glou. My Lord of Kent: remember him hereafter as   25
my honorable friend.

Edm. My services to your lordship.

Kent. I must love you, and sue to know you better.

Edm. Sir, I shall study deserving.

Glou. He hath been out nine years, and away he shall   30
again.   *Sound a sennet.*
The King is coming.

Enter *one bearing a coronet, King Lear, Cornwall,*
 Albany, Goneril, Regan, Cordelia, and *Attendants.*

Lear. Attend the lords of France and Burgundy,
Gloucester.

Glou. I shall, my lord.   35
                    [*Exeunt Gloucester and Edmund.*]

Lear. Meantime we shall express our darker purpose.
Give me the map there. Know that we have divided
In three our kingdom, and 'tis our fast intent
To shake all cares and business from our age,
Conferring them on younger strengths while we   40
Unburdened crawl toward death. Our son of Cornwall,
And you, our no less loving son of Albany,
We have this hour a constant will to publish
Our daughters' several dowers, that future strife
May be prevented now. The princes, France and Bur-   45
    gundy,

King LEAR and his Three Daughters.

Courtesy Folger Shakespeare Library

An eighteenth-century woodcut illustration for a
broadside ballad

54. **Where nature doth with merit challenge:** to
the daughter who wins it on the basis of both his affection and her own virtues

56-7. **more than word can wield the matter:** beyond the power of verbal expression

67. **champaigns:** rich plains; **riched:** enriched

73. **self:** same

75. **my very deed of love:** the exact nature of my
love

Great rivals in our youngest daughter's love,
Long in our court have made their amorous sojourn,
And here are to be answered. Tell me, my daughters
(Since now we will divest us both of rule,   50
Interest of territory, cares of state),
Which of you shall we say doth love us most?
That we our largest bounty may extend
Where nature doth with merit challenge. Goneril,
Our eldest-born, speak first.   55
    Gon. Sir, I love you more than word can wield the
      matter;
Dearer than eyesight, space, and liberty;
Beyond what can be valued, rich or rare;
No less than life, with grace, health, beauty, honor;   60
As much as child e'er loved, or father found;
A love that makes breath poor, and speech unable.
Beyond all manner of so much I love you.
    Cor. [*Aside*] What shall Cordelia speak? Love, and
      be silent.   65
    Lear. Of all these bounds, even from this line to this,
With shadowy forests and with champaigns riched,
With plenteous rivers and wide-skirted meads,
We make thee lady. To thine and Albany's issues
Be this perpetual.—What says our second daughter,   70
Our dearest Regan, wife of Cornwall? Speak.
    Reg. I am made
Of that self metal as my sister,
And prize me at her worth. In my true heart
I find she names my very deed of love,   75
Only she comes too short, that I profess
Myself an enemy to all other joys
Which the most precious square of sense possesses,

79. **felicitate:** made happy

84. **hereditary:** descendants

88. **least:** Cordelia was the youngest and apparently shorter in stature than her sisters. This is the Folio reading. The Quarto reads: "Although the last, not least," a proverbial expression in Shakespeare's time, and commonly adopted by editors. For several reasons the present editors prefer the Folio reading.

90. **to be interested:** to have a share or right in

98. **According to my bond:** according to my obligation as a daughter

106. **Happily:** it may happen.

107. **must take my plight:** shall accept my plighted troth

And find I am alone felicitate
In your dear Highness' love.   80
    Cor.   [*Aside*] Then poor Cordelia!
And yet not so, since I am sure my love's
More ponderous than my tongue.
    Lear. To thee and thine hereditary ever
Remain this ample third of our fair kingdom,   85
No less in space, validity, and pleasure
Than that conferred on Goneril.—Now, our joy,
Although our last and least; to whose young love
The vines of France and milk of Burgundy
Strive to be interessed; what can you say to draw   90
A third more opulent than your sisters? Speak.
    Cor. Nothing, my lord.
    Lear. Nothing?
    Cor. Nothing.
    Lear. Nothing will come of nothing. Speak again.   95
    Cor. Unhappy that I am, I cannot heave
My heart into my mouth. I love your Majesty
According to my bond, no more nor less.
    Lear. How, how, Cordelia? Mend your speech a little,
Lest you may mar your fortunes.   100
    Cor.   Good my lord,
You have begot me, bred me, loved me; I
Return those duties back as are right fit,
Obey you, love you, and most honor you.
Why have my sisters husbands, if they say   105
They love you all? Happily, when I shall wed,
That lord whose hand must take my plight shall carry
Half my love with him, half my care and duty.
Sure I shall never marry like my sisters,
To love my father all.   110

117. **Hecate:** a Greek goddess who controlled magic arts and was believed to rule the nocturnal activities of witches. Here and elsewhere Lear's oaths demonstrate that the scene is pagan Britain.

118. **orbs:** stars

124. **he that makes his generation messes:** the eater of his own young. Such cannibalism was attributed to wild tribes of the British Isles in pre-Christian times.

126. **as well neighbored:** as close to his affection

127. **sometime:** erstwhile, since she is now disowned

131-32. **thought to set my rest/ On her kind nursery:** expected to rely on her to comfort my old age. "To set one's rest" was a phrase from the card game primero, meaning to gamble to the full on the hand held.

137. **pride, which she calls plainness:** Lear considers that Cordelia is too arrogant to offer adequate expressions of love.

Lear. But goes thy heart with this?
Cor.   Ay, good my lord.
Lear. So young, and so untender?
Cor. So young, my lord, and true.
Lear. Let it be so! thy truth then be thy dower!   115
For, by the sacred radiance of the sun,
The mysteries of Hecate and the night;
By all the operation of the orbs
From whom we do exist and cease to be;
Here I disclaim all my paternal care,   120
Propinquity and property of blood,
And as a stranger to my heart and me
Hold thee from this for ever. The barbarous Scythian,
Or he that makes his generation messes
To gorge his appetite, shall to my bosom   125
Be as well neighbored, pitied, and relieved,
As thou my sometime daughter.
Kent.   Good my liege—
Lear. Peace, Kent!
Come not between the dragon and his wrath.   130
I loved her most, and thought to set my rest
On her kind nursery.—Hence and avoid my sight!—
So be my grave my peace as here I give
Her father's heart from her! Call France! Who stirs?
Call Burgundy! Cornwall and Albany,   135
With my two daughters' dowers digest the third;
Let pride, which she calls plainness, marry her.
I do invest you jointly with my power,
Preëminence, and all the large effects
That troop with majesty. Ourself, by monthly course,   140
With reservation of an hundred knights
By you to be sustained, shall our abode
Make with you by due turn. Only we shall retain

152. **make from the shaft:** dodge the arrow; don't let yourself be the target.

160. **Answer my life my judgment:** I would stake my life on my judgment.

163. **Reverb:** echo

170. **true blank:** white center of a target. Kent means that Lear should continue to focus his attention on him from whom he can obtain honest advice.

174. **miscreant:** faithless wretch

The name, and all th' additions to a king. The sway,
Revenue, execution of the rest,   145
Beloved sons, be yours; which to confirm,
This coronet part between you.
    Kent.   Royal Lear,
Whom I have ever honored as my king,
Loved as my father, as my master followed,   150
As my great patron thought on in my prayers—
    Lear. The bow is bent and drawn, make from the shaft.
    Kent. Let it fall rather, though the fork invade
The region of my heart! Be Kent unmannerly
When Lear is mad. What wouldst thou do, old man?   155
Thinkest thou that duty shall have dread to speak
When power to flattery bows? To plainness honor's bound
When majesty falls to folly. Reserve thy state
And in thy best consideration check
This hideous rashness. Answer my life my judgment,   160
Thy youngest daughter does not love thee least,
Nor are those empty-hearted whose low sounds
Reverb no hollowness.
    Lear.   Kent, on thy life, no more!
    Kent. My life I never held but as a pawn   165
To wage against thine enemies, nor fear to lose it,
Thy safety being motive.
    Lear.   Out of my sight!
    Kent. See better, Lear, and let me still remain
The true blank of thine eye.   170
    Lear. Now by Apollo—
    Kent.   Now by Apollo, King,
Thou swearest thy gods in vain.
    Lear.   O vassal! miscreant!
                       [Reaches for his sword.]
    Alb., Corn. Dear sir, forbear!   175

176-77. **Kill thy physician and thy fee bestow/ Upon the foul disease**: Kent suggests that Lear's judgment in treating his daughters shows that his malady (rashness) has already conquered him and he does not even wish to be cured.

180. **recreant**: traitor

182. **That**: since

186. **Our potency made good**: our authority being asserted

191. **trunk**: body

201. **approve**: make proof of

Kent. Kill thy physician and thy fee bestow
Upon the foul disease. Revoke thy gift,
Or, whilst I can vent clamor from my throat,
I'll tell thee thou dost evil.
  Lear.   Hear me, recreant!   180
On thine allegiance, hear me!
That thou hast sought to make us break our vows,
Which we durst never yet, and with strained pride
To come betwixt our sentence and our power,
Which nor our nature nor our place can bear,   185
Our potency made good, take thy reward.
Five days we do allot thee for provision
To shield thee from disasters of the world,
And on the sixth to turn thy hated back
Upon our kingdom. If, on the tenth day following,   190
Thy banished trunk be found in our dominions,
The moment is thy death. Away! By Jupiter,
This shall not be revoked.
  Kent. Fare thee well, King. Since thus thou wilt appear,   195
Freedom lives hence, and banishment is here.
[*To Cordelia*] The gods to their dear shelter take thee, maid,
That justly thinkest and hast most rightly said!
[*To Regan and Goneril*] And your large speeches may 200
your deeds approve,
That good effects may spring from words of love.
Thus Kent, O princes, bids you all adieu;
He'll shape his old course in a country new.
                Exit.

Stage Dir., **Flourish:** fanfare of trumpets

208. **What in the least:** how little

218-19. **with our displeasure pieced,/ And nothing more:** added to only by our displeasure

219. **like:** please

222. **owes:** possesses

227. **Election makes not up in such conditions:** such circumstances admit of no choice; that is, I have no choice but to refuse.

231. **I would not from your love make such a stray:** I am reluctant to damage our friendship.

Flourish. Enter *Gloucester*, with *France* and *Burgundy;*
Attendants.

   Glou. Here's France and Burgundy, my noble lord.   205
   Lear. My Lord of Burgundy,
We first address toward you, who with this king
Hath rivalled for our daughter. What in the least
Will you require in present dower with her,
Or cease your quest of love?   210
   Bur.   Most royal Majesty,
I crave no more than hath your Highness offered,
Nor will you tender less.
   Lear.   Right noble Burgundy,
When she was dear to us, we did hold her so,   215
But now her price is fallen. Sir, there she stands.
If aught within that little seeming substance,
Or all of it, with our displeasure pieced,
And nothing more, may fitly like your Grace,
She's there, and she is yours.   220
   Bur.   I know no answer.
   Lear. Will you, with those infirmities she owes,
Unfriended, new adopted to our hate,
Dowered with our curse, and strangered with our oath,
Take her, or leave her?   225
   Bur.   Pardon me, royal sir.
Election makes not up in such conditions.
   Lear. Then leave her, sir; for by the power that made
     me,
I tell you all her wealth. [*To France*] For you, great King,   230
I would not from your love make such a stray
To match you where I hate; therefore beseech you
To avert your liking a more worthier way

239. **trice:** moment

240-41. **dismantle/ So many folds of favor:** pull apart such a deep and intricately-woven affection

243. **monsters it:** only a monster would be capable of it.

243-44. **your fore-vouched affection/ Fall into taint:** your previously sworn love must be doubted.

248. **for:** because

255. **still-soliciting:** constantly begging

257. **lost me in your liking:** lost my favor with you

Than on a wretch whom nature is ashamed
Almost to acknowledge hers.   235
    France.   This is most strange,
That she whom even but now was your best object,
The argument of your praise, balm of your age,
The best, the dearest, should in this trice of time
Commit a thing so monstrous to dismantle   240
So many folds of favor. Sure her offense
Must be of such unnatural degree
That monsters it, or your fore-vouched affection
Fall into taint; which to believe of her
Must be a faith that reason without miracle   245
Should never plant in me.
    Cor.   I yet beseech your Majesty
(If for I want that glib and oily art
To speak and purpose not, since what I well intend,
I'll do it before I speak), that you make known   250
It is no vicious blot, murder, or foulness,
No unchaste action or dishonored step,
That hath deprived me of your grace and favor;
But even for want of that for which I am richer,
A still-soliciting eye, and such a tongue   255
As I am glad I have not, though not to have it
Hath lost me in your liking.
    Lear.   Better thou
Hadst not been born than not to have pleased me better.
    France. Is it but this—a tardiness in nature   260
Which often leaves the history unspoke
That it intends to do? My Lord of Burgundy,
What say you to the lady? Love's not love
When it is mingled with regards that stand
Aloof from th' entire point. Will you have her?   265
She is herself a dowry.

275. **Since that:** since
293. **grace:** favor; **benison:** blessing
296. **washed:** tearful

Bur.   Royal King,
Give but that portion which yourself proposed,
And here I take Cordelia by the hand,
Duchess of Burgundy.   270
  Lear. Nothing! I have sworn; I am firm.
  Bur. I am sorry then you have so lost a father
That you must lose a husband.
  Cor.   Peace be with Burgundy!
Since that respect and fortunes are his love,   275
I shall not be his wife.
  France. Fairest Cordelia, that art most rich, being
      poor;
Most choice, forsaken; and most loved, despised!
Thee and thy virtues here I seize upon.   280
Be it lawful I take up what's cast away.
Gods, gods! 'tis strange that from their coldest neglect
My love should kindle to inflamed respect.
Thy dowerless daughter, King, thrown to my chance,
Is queen of us, of ours, and our fair France.   285
Not all the dukes of waterish Burgundy
Can buy this unprized precious maid of me.
Bid them farewell, Cordelia, though unkind.
Thou losest here, a better where to find.
  Lear. Thou hast her, France; let her be thine; for we 290
Have no such daughter, nor shall ever see
That face of hers again. Therefore be gone
Without our grace, our love, our benison.
Come, noble Burgundy.
      Flourish. Exeunt Lear, Burgundy, [Cornwall, Albany,
                        Gloucester, and Attendants].
  France. Bid farewell to your sisters.   295
  Cor. The jewels of our father, with washed eyes
Cordelia leaves you. I know you what you are;

307. **At fortune's alms:** as a gift from fortune of trifling value

308. **well are worth the want that you have wanted:** deserve that your husband show you no more love than you have shown your father

309. **plighted:** also spelled pleated, intricately folded. "Plighted cunning" is hypocrisy.

321. **grossly:** obviously

326. **engraffed:** imbedded

And, like a sister, am most loath to call
Your faults as they are named. Love well our father.
To your professed bosoms I commit him;   300
But yet, alas, stood I within his grace,
I would prefer him to a better place!
So farewell to you both.
   Gon. Prescribe not us our duty.
   Reg.   Let your study   305
Be to content your lord, who hath received you
At fortune's alms. You have obedience scanted,
And well are worth the want that you have wanted.
   Cor. Time shall unfold what plighted cunning hides,
Who covers faults, at last with shame derides.   310
Well may you prosper!
   France.   Come, my fair Cordelia.
                 Exeunt France and Cordelia.
   Gon. Sister, it is not little I have to say of what most
nearly appertains to us both. I think our father will hence
tonight.   315
   Reg. That's most certain, and with you; next month
with us.
   Gon. You see how full of changes his age is. The observation we have made of it hath not been little. He
always loved our sister most, and with what poor judg-   320
ment he hath now cast her off appears too grossly.
   Reg. 'Tis the infirmity of his age; yet he hath ever but
slenderly known himself.
   Gon. The best and soundest of his time hath been but
rash; then must we look from his age to receive, not   325
alone the imperfections of long-engraffed condition,
but therewithal the unruly waywardness that infirm and
choleric years bring with them.

329. **unconstant starts:** capricious actions

331. **compliment:** ceremony

332. **hit together:** ally ourselves and agree on what to do

334. **this last surrender of his will but offend us:** Goneril fears that if Lear continues to exercise authority, his conversation with France may breed trouble.

336. **i' the heat:** while the iron's hot

〰〰〰〰〰〰〰〰〰〰〰〰〰〰〰〰〰〰〰〰〰〰〰

I. ii. The second scene introduces the subplot which parallels situations in the main plot and heightens the effect of the principal action. Edmund, bastard son of the Earl of Gloucester, determines to supplant his legitimate half-brother, Edgar, in his father's affections and get his lands. By means of a forged letter he makes Gloucester believe that Edgar desires his father's death so that he can come into his inheritance, and, Gloucester, as rash as Lear, believes Edmund's fabrication.

〰〰〰〰〰〰〰〰〰〰〰〰〰〰〰〰〰

3. **Stand in the plague of custom:** endure conventional decree

4. **curiosity of nations:** the finicky distinctions of human laws

5. **For that:** because

6. **Lag of:** behind (in birth); **base:** "base-born" was another term for bastard, but Edmund resents

Reg. Such unconstant starts are we like to have from
him as this of Kent's banishment. 330

Gon. There is further compliment of leave-taking between France and him. Pray you let's hit together. If our
father carry authority with such disposition as he bears,
this last surrender of his will but offend us.

Reg. We shall further think of it. 335

Gon. We must do something, and i' the heat.

Exeunt.

Scene II. [Inside Gloucester's Castle.]

Enter [*Edmund* the] *Bastard,* [a letter in his hand].

Edm. Thou, Nature, art my goddess; to thy law
My services are bound. Wherefore should I
Stand in the plague of custom and permit
The curiosity of nations to deprive me,
For that I am some twelve or fourteen moonshines 5
Lag of a brother? Why bastard? wherefore base?
When my dimensions are as well compact,
My mind as generous, and my shape as true,
As honest madam's issue? Why brand they us
With base? with baseness? bastardy? base, base? 10
Who, in the lusty stealth of nature, take
More composition and fierce quality
Than doth, within a dull, stale, tired bed,
Go to the creating a whole tribe of fops
Got 'tween asleep and wake? Well then, 15
Legitimate Edgar, I must have your land.

the implication in the word that his illegitimacy should label him inferior in quality despite his natural endowments.

17-8. **Our father's love is to the bastard Edmund/ As to the legitimate:** our father loves the bastard no less than his legitimate son.

24. **parted:** departed

25. **prescribed:** limited

26. **exhibition:** an allowance (from his daughters)

27. **Upon the gad:** on the spur of the moment

42. **to blame:** deserving of blame

45. **essay:** trial

Our father's love is to the bastard Edmund
As to the legitimate. Fine word, "legitimate"!
Well, my legitimate, if this letter speed
And my invention thrive, Edmund the base   20
Shall top the legitimate; I grow; I prosper.
Now, gods, stand up for bastards!

Enter Gloucester.

   Glou. Kent banished thus? and France in choler
     parted?
And the King gone tonight? prescribed his power?   25
Confined to exhibition? All this done
Upon the gad? Edmund, how now? What news?
   Edm. So please your lordship, none.
                         [Puts away the letter.]
   Glou. Why so earnestly seek you to put up that letter?
   Edm. I know no news, my lord.   30
   Glou. What paper were you reading?
   Edm. Nothing, my lord.
   Glou. No? What needed then that terrible dispatch of
it into your pocket? The quality of nothing hath not such
need to hide itself. Let's see. Come, if it be nothing, I   35
shall not need spectacles.
   Edm. I beseech you, sir, pardon me. It is a letter from
my brother that I have not all o'er-read; and for so much
as I have perused, I find it not fit for your o'erlooking.
   Glou. Give me the letter, sir.   40
   Edm. I shall offend, either to detain or give it. The
contents, as in part I understand them, are to blame.
   Glou. Let's see, let's see!
   Edm. I hope, for my brother's justification, he wrote
this but as an essay or taste of my virtue.   45

46-7. **This policy and reverence of age makes the world bitter to the best of our times:** the custom of deferring to age, which old men themselves have the power to perpetuate, makes the lives of young men bitter.

49. **idle and fond bondage:** a foolish slavery; "idle" and "fond" are synonymous

50-1. **who sways, not as it hath power, but as it is suffered:** whose actions are made possible not by real power but by the tolerance of those he afflicts

61. **closet:** private chamber

62. **character:** handwriting

69-70. **sounded you in this business:** tested your feelings about the matter

Glou. (*Reads*) *This policy and reverence of age makes
the world bitter to the best of our times; keeps our fortunes from us till our oldness cannot relish them. I begin
to find an idle and fond bondage in the oppression of
aged tyranny, who sways, not as it hath power, but as it*   50
*is suffered. Come to me, that of this I may speak more.
If our father would sleep till I waked him, you should
enjoy half his revenue for ever, and live the beloved of
your brother.*

                                        EDGAR.

Hum! Conspiracy? "Sleep till I waked him, you should   55
enjoy half his revenue." My son Edgar! Had he a hand
to write this? a heart and brain to breed it in? When
came you to this? Who brought it?

Edm. It was not brought me, my lord; there's the
cunning of it. I found it thrown in at the casement of my   60
closet.

Glou. You know the character to be your brother's?

Edm. If the matter were good, my lord, I durst swear
it were his; but in respect of that, I would fain think it
were not.   65

Glou. It is his.

Edm. It is his hand, my lord, but I hope his heart is
not in the contents.

Glou. Hath he never before sounded you in this business?   70

Edm. Never, my lord. But I have heard him oft maintain it to be fit that, sons at perfect age, and fathers de-
clined, the father should be as ward to the son, and the
son manage his revenue.

Glou. O villain, villain! His very opinion in the letter!   75
Abhorred villain! Unnatural, detested, brutish villain!

82. **run a certain course:** be certain of taking the right action

89. **meet:** appropriate

90. **auricular:** aural, by hearing what he says with your own ears

96-7. **wind me into him:** find out his real thoughts for me.

98-9. **I would unstate myself to be in a due resolution:** I would give up my wealth and position to know the truth.

100. **presently:** at once

103-5. **Though the wisdom of nature can reason it thus and thus, yet nature finds itself scourged by the sequent effects:** though human reason may think it can explain these phenomena, it cannot control the effect they have on human reason itself.

worse than brutish! Go, sirrah, seek him. I'll apprehend him. Abominable villain! Where is he?

Edm. I do not well know, my lord. If it shall please you to suspend your indignation against my brother till you can derive from him better testimony of his intent, you should run a certain course; where, if you violently proceed against him, mistaking his purpose, it would make a great gap in your own honor and shake in pieces the heart of his obedience. I dare pawn down my life for him that he hath writ this to feel my affection to your honor, and to no other pretense of danger.

Glou. Think you so?

Edm. If your honor judge it meet, I will place you where you shall hear us confer of this and by an auricular assurance have your satisfaction, and that without any further delay than this very evening.

Glou. He cannot be such a monster.

Edm. Nor is not, sure.

Glou. To his father, that so tenderly and entirely loves him. Heaven and earth! Edmund, seek him out; wind me into him, I pray you; frame the business after your own wisdom. I would unstate myself to be in a due resolution.

Edm. I will seek him, sir, presently, convey the business as I shall find means, and acquaint you withal.

Glou. These late eclipses in the sun and moon portend no good to us. Though the wisdom of nature can reason it thus and thus, yet nature finds itself scourged by the sequent effects. Love cools, friendship falls off, brothers divide. In cities, mutinies; in countries, discord; in palaces, treason; and the bond cracked 'twixt son and father. This villain of mine comes under the prediction;

109-10. **bias of nature:** natural inclination

113-14. **lose thee nothing:** that is, you will be rewarded.

116. **foppery:** foolishness

120-21. **treachers:** traitors

123-24. **divine thrusting on:** supernatural incitement

125. **goatish:** lustful

131. **the catastrophe:** the tragic happening which resolves all the difficulties of the plot at once

132-33. **Tom o' Bedlam:** a well-known name for a mad beggar. "Bedlam" was a corruption of Bethlehem (Hospital) which housed the insane.

there's son against father: the King falls from bias of
nature; there's father against child. We have seen the 110
best of our time. Machinations, hollowness, treachery,
and all ruinous disorders follow us disquietly to our
graves. Find out this villain, Edmund; it shall lose thee
nothing; do it carefully. And the noble and true-hearted
Kent banished! his offense, honesty! 'Tis strange. 115

Exit.

Edm. This is the excellent foppery of the world, that,
when we are sick in fortune, often the surfeits of our
own behavior, we make guilty of our disasters the sun,
the moon, and stars; as if we were villains on necessity;
fools by heavenly compulsion; knaves, thieves, and treach- 120
ers by spherical predominance; drunkards, liars, and
adulterers by an enforced obedience of planetary influence; and all that we are evil in, by a divine thrusting
on. An admirable evasion of whoremaster man, to lay his
goatish disposition to the charge of a star! My father 125
compounded with my mother under the Dragon's Tail,
and my nativity was under Ursa Major, so that it follows
I am rough and lecherous. Fut! I should have been
that I am, had the maidenliest star in the firmament
twinkled on my bastardizing. 130

Enter *Edgar.*

Pat! he comes, like the catastrophe of the old comedy.
My cue is villainous melancholy, with a sigh like Tom
o' Bedlam. O, these eclipses do portend these divisions!
Fa, sol, la, mi.

Edg. How now, brother Edmund? What serious con- 135
templation are you in?

A
DEFENCE OF IVDICI-
ALL ASTROLOGIE, IN
ANSWER TO A TREATISE
lately published by M. John Chamber

*Wherein all those places of Scripture, Councells, Fathers, Schoole-
men, later Divines, Philosophers, Histories, Lawes, Constituti-
ons, and reasons drawne out of Sixtus Empericus, Picus, Pere-
rius, Sixtus ab Heminga, and others against this Arte, are particularly examined: and the lawfulnes thereof, by equivalent
proofes warranted.*

By Sir Christopher Heydon Knight.

Seene and allowed.

PRINTED BY IOHN LEGAT, PRIN-
ter to the Vniuersitie of Cambridge. 1 6 0 3.

*And are to be sold in Pauls Churchyard at the signe of the Crowne
by Simon Waterson.*

Courtesy Folger Shakespeare Library

A contribution by Sir Christopher Heydon to the
astronomical disputes referred to in I. ii.

145. **dissipation of cohorts:** dissolution of bodies
of soldiers

147. **sectary astronomical:** a believer in the astro-
logical fads then current

153. **countenance:** general behavior

158-59. **with the mischief of your person it would
scarcely allay:** it would take more than injury of your
person to satisfy him.

17

Edm. I am thinking, brother, of a prediction I read this other day, what should follow these eclipses.

Edg. Do you busy yourself with that?

Edm. I promise you, the effects he writes of succeed 140 unhappily: as of unnaturalness between the child and the parent; death, dearth, dissolutions of ancient amities; divisions in state, menaces and maledictions against king and nobles; needless diffidences, banishment of friends, dissipation of cohorts, nuptial breaches, and I know not 145 what.

Edg. How long have you been a sectary astronomical?

Edm. When saw you my father last?

Edg. The night gone by.

Edm. Spake you with him?   150

Edg. Ay, two hours together.

Edm. Parted you in good terms? Found you no displeasure in him by word nor countenance?

Edg. None at all.

Edm. Bethink yourself wherein you may have of- 155 fended him; and at my entreaty forbear his presence until some little time hath qualified the heat of his displeasure, which at this instant so rageth in him that with the mischief of your person it would scarcely allay.

Edg. Some villain hath done me wrong.   160

Edm. That's my fear. I pray you have a continent forbearance till the speed of his rage goes slower; and, as I say, retire with me to my lodging, from whence I will fitly bring you to hear my lord speak. Pray ye, go! There's my key. If you do stir abroad, go armed.   165

Edg. Armed, brother?

Edm. Brother, I advise you to the best. I am no honest man if there be any good meaning toward you. I have

176. **practices:** stratagems

178. **All with me's meet that I can fashion fit:** any trick suits me that will further my purposes.

‖‖

I. iii. Some days later. Lear is spending his time with Goneril, wife of the Duke of Albany. Her father's petulance and the riotousness of his knights have displeased her, and she instructs her steward, Oswald, to be so negligent of the King that he will complain to her and give her the opportunity to bring him to terms.

‖‖‖‖‖‖‖‖‖‖‖‖‖‖‖‖‖‖‖‖‖‖‖‖‖‖‖‖‖‖‖‖‖‖‖

8. **On:** because of

10. **come slack of former services:** offer less service than formerly

told you what I have seen and heard; but faintly, nothing
like the image and horror of it. Pray you, away!

  Edg. Shall I hear from you anon?   170
  Edm. I do serve you in this business.

                              Exit Edgar.

A credulous father! and a brother noble,
Whose nature is so far from doing harms
That he suspects none; on whose foolish honesty   175
My practices ride easy! I see the business.
Let me, if not by birth, have lands by wit;
All with me's meet that I can fashion fit.   *Exit.*

Scene III. [Inside the Duke of Albany's Palace.]

Enter *Goneril* and [*Oswald,* her] *Steward.*

  Gon. Did my father strike my gentleman for chiding of
    his fool?
  Osw. Ay, madam.
  Gon. By day and night, he wrongs me! Every hour
He flashes into one gross crime or other   5
That sets us all at odds. I'll not endure it.
His knights grow riotous, and himself upbraids us
On every trifle. When he returns from hunting,
I will not speak with him. Say I am sick.
If you come slack of former services,   10
You shall do well; the fault of it I'll answer.

                        [Horns within.]

  Osw. He's coming, madam; I hear him.

14. **I'd have it come to question:** I would like to provoke an open quarrel.

17. **Idle:** foolish; see I. ii. 49.

20-1. **must be used/ With checks as flatteries, when they are seen abused:** must be corrected instead of flattered when they appear deluded

26. **breed from hence occasions:** create opportunities (for a clash with Lear)

||||||||||||||||||||||||||||||||||||||||||||||||||||||||||

I. iv. This scene reveals that Lear realizes his folly in giving away his possessions. Kent returns in disguise to serve him. The Fool is introduced for the first time and his commentary serves to heighten Lear's own realization of his plight. By reducing the number of his servingmen and further humiliating him, Goneril drives Lear into a fury and induces him to turn to Regan.

||||||||||||||||||||||||||||||||||||||||||||

2. **diffuse:** disorder

4. **razed my likeness:** destroyed my natural appearance

Gon. Put on what weary negligence you please,
You and your fellows. I'd have it come to question.
If he distaste it, let him to my sister,   15
Whose mind and mine I know in that are one,
Not to be overruled. Idle old man,
That still would manage those authorities
That he hath given away! Now, by my life,
Old fools are babes again, and must be used   20
With checks as flatteries, when they are seen abused.
Remember what I have said.
   Osw.   Very well, madam.
   Gon. And let his knights have colder looks among you.
What grows of it, no matter. Advise your fellows so.   25
I would breed from hence occasions, and I shall,
That I may speak. I'll write straight to my sister
To hold my very course. Prepare for dinner.
                            Exeunt.

Scene IV. [Inside the Duke of Albany's Palace.]

Enter *Kent*, [disguised].

Kent. If but as well I other accents borrow,
That can my speech diffuse, my good intent
May carry through itself to that full issue
For which I razed my likeness. Now, banished Kent,
If thou canst serve where thou dost stand condemned,   5
So may it come, thy master, whom thou lovest,
Shall find thee full of labors.

Stage Dir., **Horns within**: hunting horns announce Lear's return.

11. **profess**: work at

17. **eat no fish**: an anachronistic allusion to the laws requiring the faithful to eat fish on Friday

27. **countenance**: behavior; see I. ii. 153.

33. **curious**: intricate

Horns within. Enter *Lear*, [*Knights*,] and *Attendants.*

Lear. Let me not stay a jot for dinner; go get it ready.
[*Exit an Attendant.*] How now? What art thou?

Kent. A man, sir.   10

Lear. What dost thou profess? What wouldst thou
with us?

Kent. I do profess to be no less than I seem, to serve
him truly that will put me in trust, to love him that is
honest, to converse with him that is wise and says little,   15
to fear judgment, to fight when I cannot choose, and to
eat no fish.

Lear. What art thou?

Kent. A very honest-hearted fellow, and as poor as the
King.   20

Lear. If thou be'st as poor for a subject as he is for a
king, thou art poor enough. What wouldst thou?

Kent. Service.

Lear. Who wouldst thou serve?

Kent. You.   25

Lear. Dost thou know me, fellow?

Kent. No, sir, but you have that in your countenance
which I would fain call master.

Lear. What's that?

Kent. Authority.   30

Lear. What services canst thou do?

Kent. I can keep honest counsel, ride, run, mar a
curious tale in telling it, and deliver a plain message
bluntly. That which ordinary men are fit for, I am qualified in, and the best of me is diligence.   35

Lear. How old art thou?

Kent. Not so young, sir, to love a woman for singing,

46. **clotpoll**: blockhead

53. **roundest**: bluntest

nor so old to dote on her for anything. I have years on
my back forty-eight.

 Lear. Follow me; thou shalt serve me. If I like thee no 40
worse after dinner, I will not part from thee yet. Dinner,
ho, dinner! Where's my knave? my fool? Go you and call
my fool hither.

           [*Exit an Attendant.*]

    Enter [*Oswald* the] *Steward.*

You, you, sirrah, where's my daughter?

 Osw. So please you—   *Exit.* 45

 Lear. What says the fellow there? Call the clotpoll
back. [*Exit a Knight.*] Where's my fool, ho? I think the
world's asleep.

    [Enter *Knight.*]

How now? Where's that mongrel?

 Knight. He says, my lord, your daughter is not well. 50

 Lear. Why came not the slave back to me when I
called him?

 Knight. Sir, he answered me in the roundest manner,
he would not.

 Lear. He would not?   . 55

 Knight. My lord, I know not what the matter is, but
to my judgment your Highness is not entertained with
that ceremonious affection as you were wont. There's a
great abatement of kindness appears as well in the general dependants as in the Duke himself also and your 60
daughter.

66. **rememberest**: reminds

68-9. **jealous curiosity**: suspicious and finicky vigilance

83. **bandy**: toss back and forth (as though he were Lear's equal)

85. **base football player**: football was a game played by the lower classes.

Lear. Ha! sayest thou so?

Knight. I beseech you pardon me, my lord, if I be mistaken, for my duty cannot be silent when I think your Highness wronged.   65

Lear. Thou but rememberest me of mine own conception. I have perceived a most faint neglect of late, which I have rather blamed as mine own jealous curiosity than as a very pretense and purpose of unkindness. I will look further into it. But where's my fool? I have   70 not seen him this two days.

Knight. Since my young lady's going into France, sir, the fool hath much pined away.

Lear. No more of that; I have noted it well. Go you and tell my daughter I would speak with her. [*Exit*   75 *Knight.*] Go you, call hither my fool.

                           [*Exit an Attendant.*]

           [Re-] Enter *Steward.*

O, you, sir, you! Come you hither, sir. Who am I, sir?

Osw. My lady's father.

Lear. "My lady's father"? My lord's knave! You whoreson dog! you slave! you cur!   80

Osw. I am none of these, my lord! I beseech your pardon.

Lear. Do you bandy looks with me, you rascal?

                           [*Strikes him.*]

Osw. I'll not be strucken, my lord.

Kent. Nor tripped neither, you base football player?   85

                           [*Trips him.*]

Lear. I thank thee, fellow. Thou servest me, and I'll love thee.

88. **differences:** the proper evaluation of your status in relation to others

89. **lubber:** a clumsy person

90. **Go to:** be off; **Have you wisdom:** i.e., common sense; do you know what's good for you

92. **earnest:** a partial payment in advance to seal an agreement

93. **coxcomb:** a clown's cap, conventionally shaped like a cock's comb

98-9. **an thou canst not smile as the wind sits, thou'lt catch cold:** if you can't agree with those in control, it will be the worse for you.

100. **on's:** of his

102. **nuncle:** uncle, shortened from "mine uncle"

108. **the whip:** fools were punished by whipping when they offended their patrons.

109-11. **Truth's a dog must to kennel; he must be whipped out, when the Lady Brach may stand by the fire and stink:** "brach" was a term for a hound bitch. The comparison is between truth and fawning flattery like that of a petted bitch. Many editors emend the Folio reading to "Lady the brach" on the basis that "Lady" was a popular name for pet brachs.

112. **A pestilent gall to me:** Lear is presumably commenting on the bitterness of the Fool's quips.

Kent. Come, sir, arise, away! I'll teach you differences. Away, away! If you will measure your lubber's length again, tarry; but away! Go to! Have you wisdom? So.   90
[*Exit Oswald.*]

Lear. Now, my friendly knave, I thank thee.

Enter *Fool.*

There's earnest of thy service.   [*Gives Kent money.*]

Fool. Let me hire him too. Here's my coxcomb.
[*Offers Kent his cap.*]

Lear. How now, my pretty knave? How dost thou?

Fool. Sirrah, you were best take my coxcomb.   95

Kent. Why, fool?

Fool. Why? For taking one's part that's out of favor. Nay, an thou canst not smile as the wind sits, thou'lt catch cold shortly. There, take my coxcomb! Why, this fellow has banished two on's daughters, and did the   100 third a blessing against his will. If thou follow him, thou must needs wear my coxcomb.—How now, nuncle? Would I had two coxcombs and two daughters!

Lear. Why, my boy?

Fool. If I gave them all my living, I'd keep my cox-   105 combs myself. There's mine! beg another of thy daughters.

Lear. Take heed, sirrah—the whip.

Fool. Truth's a dog must to kennel; he must be whipped out, when the Lady Brach may stand by the   110 fire and stink.

Lear. A pestilent gall to me!

Fool. Sirrah, I'll teach thee a speech.

Lear. Do.

A fool and a courtesan.
From Robert Greene's *The Third . . .
Part of Conny Catching* (1592)

118. **owest:** ownest; see I. i. 222.

119. **goest:** that is, on foot

120. **Learn more than thou trowest:** don't mistake guesses for facts.

121. **Set less than thou throwest:** don't stake all your winnings on the next throw of dice.

127. **unfeed:** unpaid

132-33. **so much the rent of his land comes to:** since Lear has given his land away, it is no longer a source of income to him.

144. **motley:** the multicolored garb of a fool

Fool. Mark it, nuncle. 115

> Have more than thou showest,
> Speak less than thou knowest,
> Lend less than thou owest,
> Ride more than thou goest,
> Learn more than thou trowest, 120
> Set less than thou throwest;
> Leave thy drink and thy whore,
> And keep in-a-door,
> And thou shalt have more
> Than two tens to a score. 125

Kent. This is nothing, fool.

Fool. Then 'tis like the breath of an unfeed lawyer—you gave me nothing for it. Can you make no use of nothing, nuncle?

Lear. Why, no, boy. Nothing can be made out of 130 nothing.

Fool. [*To Kent*] Prithee tell him, so much the rent of his land comes to. He will not believe a fool.

Lear. A bitter fool!

Fool. Dost thou know the difference, my boy, between 135 a bitter fool and a sweet one?

Lear. No, lad; teach me.

Fool.
> That lord that counselled thee
>> To give away thy land,
> Come place him here by me— 140
>> Do thou for him stand.
> The sweet and bitter fool
>> Will presently appear;
> The one in motley here,
>> The other found out there. 145

Lear. Dost thou call me fool, boy?

149. **This is not altogether fool**: that is, there is some wit in what he says. The Fool pretends to misunderstand and replies that he has no monopoly of foolery.

151. **monopoly**: a reference to the current abuses of monopolies granted to courtiers by the King; **on't**: of it

159. **borest thine ass on thy back o'er the dirt**: a reference to the fable of Aesop

161-62. **If I speak like myself in this, let him be whipped that first finds it so**: if I speak foolishly, whip the man who first realizes that I have spoken truth.

163-64. **Fools had ne'er less grace in a year,/ For wise men are grown foppish**: fools are valued little at present because too many wise men behave foolishly.

166. **apish**: foolishly affected

174-75. **play bo-peep/ And go the fools among**: hide his royalty in behaving like a fool

Fool. All thy other titles thou hast given away; that thou wast born with.

Kent. This is not altogether fool, my lord.

Fool. No, faith; lords and great men will not let me. 150 If I had a monopoly out, they would have part on't. And ladies too, they will not let me have all the fool to myself; they'll be snatching. Nuncle, give me an egg, and I'll give thee two crowns.

Lear. What two crowns shall they be?   155

Fool. Why, after I have cut the egg i' the middle and eat up the meat, the two crowns of the egg. When thou clovest thy crown i' the middle and gavest away both parts, thou borest thine ass on thy back o'er the dirt. Thou hadst little wit in thy bald crown when thou gavest 160 thy golden one away. If I speak like myself in this, let him be whipped that first finds it so.

[*Sings*]   Fools had ne'er less grace in a year,
                        For wise men are grown foppish;
                        And know not how their wits to wear,   165
                        Their manners are so apish.

Lear. When were you wont to be so full of songs, sirrah?

Fool. I have used it, nuncle, ever since thou madest thy daughters thy mother; for when thou gavest them the 170 rod, and puttest down thine own breeches,

[*Sings*]   Then they for sudden joy did weep,
                        And I for sorrow sung,
                        That such a king should play bo-peep
                        And go the fools among.   175

Prithee, nuncle, keep a schoolmaster that can teach thy fool to lie. I would fain learn to lie.

Lear. An you lie, sirrah, we'll have you whipped.

186. **What makes**: what is the purpose of; **frontlet**: a forehead band

189. **an O**: a zero

196. **shealed**: shelled

204. **put it on**: encourage it

205-10. **the fault . . . proceeding**: the misdemeanor would not go uncriticized nor unpunished in the interest of a harmonious state, perhaps in a manner that would seem a shameful abuse of you were it not that discretion made it necessary.

Fool. I marvel what kin thou and thy daughters are.
They'll have me whipped for speaking true; thou'lt have 180
me whipped for lying; and sometimes I am whipped for
holding my peace. I had rather be any kind o' thing than
a fool! And yet I would not be thee, nuncle. Thou hast
pared thy wit o' both sides and left nothing i' the middle.
Here comes one o' the parings. 185

Enter *Goneril.*

Lear. How now, daughter? What makes that frontlet
on? You are too much o' late i' the frown.
Fool. Thou wast a pretty fellow when thou hadst no
need to care for her frowning. Now thou art an O without
a figure. I am better than thou art now: I am a fool, thou 190
art nothing. [*To Goneril*] Yes, forsooth, I will hold my
tongue. So your face bids me, though you say nothing.
Mum, mum!

> He that keeps nor crust nor crum,
>   Weary of all, shall want some.— 195

[*Pointing at Lear*] That's a shealed peascod.
Gon. Not only, sir, this your all-licensed fool,
But other of your insolent retinue
Do hourly carp and quarrel, breaking forth
In rank and not-to-be-endured riots. Sir, 200
I had thought, by making this well known unto you,
To have found a safe redress; but now grow fearful,
By what yourself too late have spoke and done,
That you protect this course, and put it on
By your allowance; which if you should, the fault 205
Would not scape censure, nor the redresses sleep,
Which, in the tender of a wholesome weal,

213. **it**: its. The Fool is talking baby talk.

217. **fraught**: freighted, full

218. **dispositions**: capricious humors

221. **Jug**: a common diminutive for "Joan" and a general form of address to a sweetheart

224. **notion**: understanding

234. **admiration**: wonder; that is, "your pretense of wonder"

Might in their working do you that offense
Which else were shame, that then necessity
Must call discreet proceeding.   210
  Fool. For you know, nuncle,
        The hedge-sparrow fed the cuckoo so long
        That it's had it head bit off by it young.
So out went the candle, and we were left darkling.
  Lear. Are you our daughter?   215
  Gon. I would you would make use of your good wisdom,
Whereof I know you are fraught, and put away
These dispositions which of late transport you
From what you rightly are.
  Fool. May not an ass know when the cart draws the 220
horse? Whoop, Jug, I love thee!
  Lear. Does any here know me? This is not Lear.
Does Lear walk thus? speak thus? Where are his eyes?
Either his notion weakens, or his discernings
Are lethargied—Sleeping or waking? Ha! Sure 'tis not so! 225
Who is it that can tell me who I am?
  Fool. Lear's shadow.
  Lear. I would learn that; for, by the marks of sover-
        eignty,
Knowledge, and reason, I should be false persuaded   230
I had daughters.
  Fool. Which they will make an obedient father.
  Lear. Your name, fair gentlewoman?
  Gon. This admiration, sir, is much o' the savor
Of other your new pranks. I do beseech you   235
To understand my purposes aright.
As you are old and reverend, you should be wise.
Here do you keep a hundred knights and squires;
Men so disordered, so debauched, and bold
That this our court, infected with their manners,   240

247. **depend**: serve as dependants
248. **besort**: suit
257. **Woe**: i.e., "woe to him."
267. **worships**: honor
269. **engine**: machine

Shows like a riotous inn. Epicurism and lust
Make it more like a tavern or a brothel
Than a graced palace. The shame itself doth speak
For instant remedy. Be then desired
By her that else will take the thing she begs   245
A little to disquantity your train,
And the remainders that shall still depend
To be such men as may besort your age,
Which know themselves and you.
  Lear.   Darkness and devils!   250
Saddle my horses! Call my train together!
Degenerate bastard, I'll not trouble thee;
Yet have I left a daughter.
  Gon. You strike my people, and your disordered
    rabble   255
Make servants of their betters.

Enter *Albany.*

  Lear. Woe that too late repents!—O, sir, are you come?
Is it your will? Speak, sir!—Prepare my horses.
Ingratitude, thou marble-hearted fiend,
More hideous when thou showest thee in a child   260
Than the sea-monster!
  Alb.   Pray, sir, be patient.
  Lear. [*To Goneril*] Detested kite, thou liest!
My train are men of choice and rarest parts,
That all particulars of duty know   265
And in the most exact regard support
The worships of their name.—O most small fault,
How ugly didst thou in Cordelia show!
Which, like an engine, wrenched my frame of nature
From the fixed place; drew from my heart all love   270

282. **derogate**: debased
287. **cadent**: falling

And added to the gall. O Lear, Lear, Lear!
Beat at this gate that let thy folly in
           [*Beats his forehead with his fist.*]
And thy dear judgment out! Go, go, my people.
  Alb. My lord, I am guiltless, as I am ignorant
Of what hath moved you.   275
  Lear.   It may be so, my lord.
Hear, Nature, hear! dear goddess, hear!
Suspend thy purpose, if thou didst intend
To make this creature fruitful.
Into her womb convey sterility;   280
Dry up in her the organs of increase;
And from her derogate body never spring
A babe to honor her! If she must teem,
Create her child of spleen, that it may live
And be a thwart disnatured torment to her.   285
Let it stamp wrinkles in her brow of youth,
With cadent tears fret channels in her cheeks,
Turn all her mother's pains and benefits
To laughter and contempt, that she may feel
How sharper than a serpent's tooth it is   290
To have a thankless child! Away, away!   *Exit.*
  Alb. Now, gods that we adore, whereof comes this?
  Gon. Never afflict yourself to know more of it,
But let his disposition have that scope
As dotage gives it.   295

           [Re-] Enter *Lear*.

  Lear. What, fifty of my followers at a clap?
Within a fortnight?
  Alb.   What's the matter, sir?

304. **untented**: too deep to be reached with a probe (a "tent")

325. **Should sure to**: would surely go to

326. **halter**: hangman's noose

Lear. I'll tell thee. [*To Goneril*] Life and death! I am
   ashamed   300
That thou hast power to shake my manhood thus;
That these hot tears, which break from me perforce,
Should make thee worth them. Blasts and fogs upon thee!
Th' untented woundings of a father's curse
Pierce every sense about thee!—Old fond eyes,   305
Beweep this cause again, I'll pluck ye out,
And cast you, with the waters that you loose,
To temper clay. Yea, is it come to this?
Ha! Let it be so. I have another daughter,
Who I am sure is kind and comfortable.   310
When she shall hear this of thee, with her nails
She'll flay thy wolvish visage. Thou shalt find
That I'll resume the shape which thou dost think
I have cast off for ever.
             Exeunt [*Lear, Kent, and Attendants*].
   Gon. Do you mark that, my lord?   315
   Alb. I cannot be so partial, Goneril,
To the great love I bear you—
   Gon. Pray you, content.—What, Oswald, ho!
[*To the Fool*] You, sir, more knave than fool, after your
   master!   320
   Fool. Nuncle Lear, nuncle Lear, tarry! Take the fool
with thee.

         A fox, when one has caught her,
         And such a daughter,
         Should sure to the slaughter,   325
         If my cap would buy a halter.
         So the fool follows after.   *Exit.*
   Gon. This man hath had good counsel! A hundred
   knights?
'Tis politic and safe to let him keep   330

331. **At point**: fully equipped with arms
334. **in mercy**: at his mercy
337. **still**: always
346. **particular**: personal
348. **compact it more**: add to its substance
357. **the event**: that is, "we'll see what will happen."

At point a hundred knights; yes, that on every dream,
Each buzz, each fancy, each complaint, dislike,
He may enguard his dotage with their powers
And hold our lives in mercy.—Oswald, I say!
  Alb. Well, you may fear too far.   335
  Gon.   Safer than trust too far.
Let me still take away the harms I fear,
Not fear still to be taken. I know his heart.
What he hath uttered I have writ my sister.
If she sustain him and his hundred knights.   340
When I have showed the unfitness—

Enter *Steward.*

                    How now, Oswald?
What, have you writ that letter to my sister?
  Osw. Yes, madam.
  Gon. Take you some company, and away to horse!   345
Inform her full of my particular fear,
And thereto add such reasons of your own
As may compact it more. Get you gone,
And hasten your return. [*Exit Oswald.*] No, no, my lord!
This milky gentleness and course of yours,   350
Though I condemn not, yet, under pardon,
You are much more at task for want of wisdom
Than praised for harmful mildness.
  Alb. How far your eyes may pierce I cannot tell.
Striving to better, oft we mar what's well.   355
  Gon. Nay then—
  Alb. Well, well; the event.

                        Exeunt.

I. v. Lear departs for Regan's domain as the Fool comments on his folly.

||||||||||||||||||||||||||||||||||||||

8. **kibes**: chilblains

10-11. **Thy wit shall not go slipshod**: you will never need to wear loose slippers (go slipshod) to protect your chilblained wits, because you have none.

14. **crab**: crabapple

21. **side's**: side of his

Scene V. [A courtyard of the Duke of
Albany's Palace.]

Enter *Lear*, *Kent*, and *Fool*.

Lear. Go you before to Gloucester with these letters.
Acquaint my daughter no further with anything you
know than comes from her demand out of the letter. If
your diligence be not speedy, I shall be there afore you.

Kent. I will not sleep, my lord, till I have delivered   5
your letter.   *Exit.*

Fool. If a man's brains were in's heels, were it not in
danger of kibes?

Lear. Ay, boy.

Fool. Then I prithee be merry. Thy wit shall not go   10
slipshod.

Lear. Ha, ha, ha!

Fool. Shalt see thy other daughter will use thee kind-
ly; for though she's as like this as a crab's like an apple,
yet I can tell what I can tell.   15

Lear. What canst tell, boy?

Fool. She'll taste as like this as a crab does to a crab.
Thou canst tell why one's nose stands i' the middle on's
face?

Lear. No.   20

Fool. Why, to keep one's eyes of either side's nose,
that what a man cannot smell out, he may spy into.

Lear. I did her wrong.

Fool. Canst tell how an oyster makes his shell?

Lear. No.   25

29. **put's**: put his
34. **seven stars**: the Pleiades; **mo**: more

Fool. Nor I neither; but I can tell why a snail has a house.

Lear. Why?

Fool. Why, to put's head in; not to give it away to his daughters, and leave his horns without a case. 30

Lear. I will forget my nature. So kind a father!—Be my horses ready?

Fool. Thy asses are gone about 'em. The reason why the seven stars are no mo than seven is a pretty reason.

Lear. Because they are not eight? 35

Fool. Yes indeed. Thou wouldst make a good fool.

Lear. To take it again perforce! Monster ingratitude!

Fool. If thou wert my fool, nuncle, I'd have thee beaten for being old before thy time.

Lear. How's that? 40

Fool. Thou shouldst not have been old till thou hadst been wise.

Lear. O, let me not be mad, not mad, sweet heaven! Keep me in temper; I would not be mad!

[Enter a *Gentleman*.]

How now? Are the horses ready? 45

Gent. Ready, my lord.

Lear. Come, boy.

Fool. She that's a maid now, and laughs at my departure,

Shall not be a maid long, unless things be cut shorter. 50
                                                Exeunt.

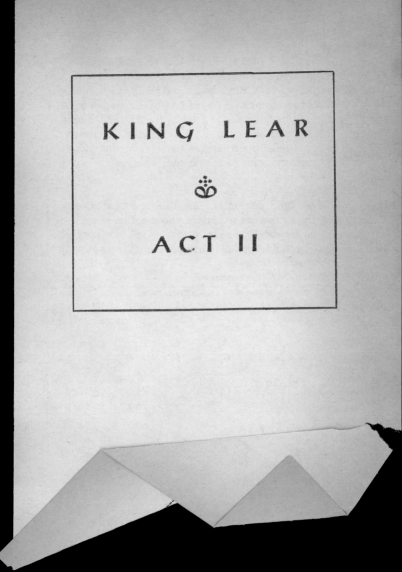

KING LEAR

ACT II

II. i. In the opening scene of Act II, Shakespeare begins to weave the subplot and the main plot together. Edmund hoodwinks Edgar into fleeing to escape Gloucester's anger and contrives the appearance of a murderous assault on himself by Edgar when he would not assist in the murder of their father. Regan and the Duke of Cornwall come to visit Gloucester, and Edmund supports Regan's statement that Edgar had consorted with Lear's "riotous knights."

Stage Dir., **severally:** i.e., Edmund and Curan come from different directions and meet on stage.

8. **ear-bussing:** ear-kissing; that is, not spoken aloud but whispered surreptitiously; **arguments:** summaries of facts

10. **toward:** in prospect

17. **queasy question:** ticklish nature

ACT II

Scene I. [A courtyard inside Gloucester's Castle.]

Enter [Edmund the] Bastard and Curan, severally.

Edm. Save thee, Curan.

Cur. And you, sir. I have been with your father, and given him notice that the Duke of Cornwall and Regan his Duchess will be here with him this night.

Edm. How comes that? 5

Cur. Nay, I know not. You have heard of the news abroad—I mean the whispered ones, for they are yet but ear-bussing arguments?

Edm. Not I. Pray you, what are they?

Cur. Have you heard of no likely wars toward 'twixt 10 the Dukes of Cornwall and Albany?

Edm. Not a word.

Cur. You may do, then, in time. Fare you well, sir.

Exit.

Edm. The Duke be here tonight? The better! best!
This weaves itself perforce into my business. 15
My father hath set guard to take my brother;
And I have one thing, of a queasy question,
Which I must act. Briefness and fortune, work!
Brother, a word! Descend! Brother, I say!

34

27. **Advise yourself**: reflect on what your situation is.

30. **In cunning**: in pretense

31. **quit you well**: defend yourself

34-5. **beget opinion/ Of my more fierce endeavor**: indicate a fierce struggle

42. **stand auspicious mistress**: sponsor his fortunes

Enter *Edgar*.

My father watches. O sir, fly this place!   20
Intelligence is given where you are hid.
You have now the good advantage of the night.
Have you not spoken 'gainst the Duke of Cornwall?
He's coming hither; now, i' the night, i' the haste,
And Regan with him. Have you nothing said   25
Upon his party 'gainst the Duke of Albany?
Advise yourself.
 Edg.   I am sure on't, not a word.
 Edm. I hear my father coming. Pardon me!
In cunning I must draw my sword upon you.   30
Draw, seem to defend yourself; now quit you well.—
Yield! Come before my father. Light, ho, here!
Fly, brother.—Torches, torches!—So farewell.
           Exit Edgar.

Some blood drawn on me would beget opinion
Of my more fierce endeavor. [*Stabs his arm.*] I have seen   35
 drunkards
Do more than this in sport.—Father, father!—
Stop, stop! No help?

Enter *Gloucester*, and *Servants* with torches.

 Glou. Now, Edmund, where's the villain?
 Edm. Here stood he in the dark, his sharp sword out,   40
Mumbling of wicked charms, conjuring the moon
To stand auspicious mistress.
 Glou.   But where is he?
 Edm. Look, sir, I bleed.
 Glou.   Where is the villain, Edmund?   45

55. **fell:** fierce

57. **unprovided:** undefended; **lanched:** lanced

60. **gasted:** terrified

64. **And found—dispatch:** that is, he will be killed on sight.

65. **arch and patron:** principal patron

71. **pight:** determined; **curst:** angry

72. **discover:** denounce

76. **faithed:** credited

78. **character:** handwriting; see I. ii. 62.

Edm. Fled this way, sir. When by no means he could—
Glou. Pursue him, ho! Go after. [*Exeunt some Serv-
   ants.*] By no means what?
Edm. Persuade me to the murder of your lordship;
But that I told him the revenging gods   50
'Gainst parricides did all the thunder bend;
Spoke with how manifold and strong a bond
The child was bound to the father—sir, in fine,
Seeing how loathly opposite I stood
To his unnatural purpose, in fell motion   55
With his prepared sword he charges home
My unprovided body, lanched mine arm;
And when he saw my best alarumed spirits,
Bold in the quarrel's right, roused to the encounter,
Or whether gasted by the noise I made,   60
Full suddenly he fled.
Glou.   Let him fly far.
Not in this land shall he remain uncaught;
And found—dispatch. The noble Duke my master,
My worthy arch and patron, comes tonight.   65
By his authority I will proclaim it,
That he which finds him shall deserve our thanks,
Bringing the murderous coward to the stake;
He that conceals him, death.
Edm. When I dissuaded him from his intent   70
And found him pight to do it, with curst speech
I threatened to discover him. He replied,
"Thou unpossessing bastard, dost thou think,
If I would stand against thee, would the reposal
Of any trust, virtue, or worth in thee   75
Make thy words faithed? No. What I should deny
(As this I would; ay, though thou didst produce
My very character), I'd turn it all

79. **practice:** trick, stratagem; see I. ii. 176.

81. **not thought:** i.e., did not think

84. **strange:** unnatural (in planning the murder of his own father); **fastened:** hardened, confirmed

Stage Dir., **Tucket:** a flourish of trumpets, usually the signal for troops to march

91. **natural:** Edmund is a "natural" child, i.e., illegitimate, and he behaves according to nature's rules in showing devotion to his father. Gloucester probably has both meanings in mind.

92. **capable:** of inheriting Gloucester's estate; in other words, Gloucester is promising to legalize Edmund's position as his heir.

105. **though:** if; **ill affected:** disaffected (toward his father)

To thy suggestion, plot, and damned practice;
And thou must make a dullard of the world,　　　　　80
If they not thought the profits of my death
Were very pregnant and potential spirits
To make thee seek it."
　　Glou.　　　　　　　O strange and fastened villain!
Would he deny his letter, said he? I never got him.　　85
　　　　　　　　　　　　　　　Tucket within.
Hark, the Duke's trumpets! I know not why he comes.
All ports I'll bar; the villain shall not scape;
The Duke must grant me that. Besides, his picture
I will send far and near, that all the kingdom
May have due note of him, and of my land,　　　　　90
Loyal and natural boy, I'll work the means
To make thee capable.

Enter *Cornwall, Regan* and *Attendants.*

　　Corn. How now, my noble friend? Since I came hither
(Which I can call but now) I have heard strange news.
　　Reg. If it be true, all vengeance comes too short　　95
Which can pursue the offender. How dost, my lord?
　　Glou. O madam, my old heart is cracked, it's cracked!
　　Reg. What, did my father's godson seek your life?
He whom my father named? Your Edgar?
　　Glou. O lady, lady, shame would have it hid!　　　100
　　Reg. Was he not companion with the riotous knights
That tended upon my father?
　　Glou. I know not, madam. 'Tis too bad, too bad!
　　Edm. Yes, madam, he was of that consort.
　　Reg. No marvel then though he were ill affected.　　105
'Tis they have put him on the old man's death,
To have the expense and waste of his revenues.

116. **bewray:** expose

121. **Be feared of doing harm:** be a danger

121-22. **Make your own purpose,/ How in my strength you please:** you may rely on my support in dealing with the matter as you think best.

128. **Truly, however else:** faithfully, though making no claims for the worth of my service

136. **from:** away from

140. **craves the instant use:** is of immediate importance

I have this present evening from my sister
Been well informed of them, and with such cautions
That, if they come to sojourn at my house,   110
I'll not be there.
    Corn.   Nor I, assure thee, Regan.
Edmund, I hear that you have shown your father
A childlike office.
    Edm.   'Twas my duty, sir.   115
    Glou. He did bewray his practice, and received
This hurt you see, striving to apprehend him.
    Corn. Is he pursued?
    Glou.   Ay, my good lord.
    Corn. If he be taken, he shall never more   120
Be feared of doing harm. Make your own purpose,
How in my strength you please. For you, Edmund,
Whose virtue and obedience doth this instant
So much commend itself, you shall be ours.
Natures of such deep trust we shall much need;   125
You we first seize on.
    Edm.   I shall serve you, sir,
Truly, however else.
    Glou.   For him I thank your Grace.
    Corn. You know not why we came to visit you—   130
    Reg. Thus out of season, threading dark-eyed night.
Occasions, noble Gloucester, of some prize,
Wherein we must have use of your advice.
Our father he hath writ, so hath our sister,
Of differences, which I best thought it fit   135
To answer from our home. The several messengers
From hence attend dispatch. Our good old friend,
Lay comforts to your bosom, and bestow
Your needful counsel to our businesses,
Which craves the instant use.   140

II. ii. For abusing Oswald, Kent is placed in the stocks, an indignity to the King's messenger that is intended to humiliate Lear.

▯▯▯▯▯▯▯▯▯▯▯▯▯▯▯▯▯▯▯▯▯▯▯▯▯

8. **Lipsbury Pinfold:** "Lipsbury" means "Liptown." A pinfold was an enclosure for stray cattle. Hence: "Lipsbury Pinfold" means "in my jaws," "in my power."

15. **worsted-stocking knave:** a taunt at Oswald's low status; gentlemen wore silk stockings.

15-6. **action-taking:** too cowardly to defend himself if physically attacked, he would take legal action against his assailant.

16. **superserviceable:** willing to serve his master beyond honorable limits

17. **finical:** finicky about details; **one-trunk-inheriting:** "inheriting" means "owning"; therefore, of meager estate

22. **thy addition:** thy designations

Glou.   I serve you, madam.
Your Graces are right welcome.

> *Exeunt. Flourish.*

Scene II. [Without the gates of Gloucester's Castle.]

Enter *Kent* and [*Oswald* the] *Steward,* severally.

Osw. Good dawning to thee, friend. Art of this house?
Kent. Ay.
Osw. Where may we set our horses?
Kent. I' the mire.
Osw. Prithee, if thou lovest me, tell me.   5
Kent. I love thee not.
Osw. Why then, I care not for thee.
Kent. If I had thee in Lipsbury Pinfold, I would make
thee care for me.
Osw. Why dost thou use me thus? I know thee not.   10
Kent. Fellow, I know thee.
Osw. What dost thou know me for?
Kent. A knave, a rascal, an eater of broken meats; a
base, proud, shallow, beggarly, three-suited, hundred-
pound, filthy, worsted-stocking knave; a lily-livered, ac-   15
tion-taking, whoreson, glass-gazing, superserviceable,
finical rogue; one-trunk-inheriting slave; one that wouldst
be a bawd in way of good service, and art nothing but
the composition of a knave, beggar, coward, pander, and
the son and heir of a mongrel bitch; one whom I will   20
beat into clamorous whining if thou deny'st the least
syllable of thy addition.

24. **rail on:** scold

25. **varlet:** a low rascal

29-30. **make a sop o' the moonshine of you:** puncture you so that your body sops up the moonlight

30. **cullionly:** of a despicable character, base; **barbermonger:** one who patronizes barbers, by implication here a dandified fellow

33. **Vanity the puppet:** Lady Vanity was a character common in morality plays, which were often presented as puppet shows. Kent refers here to Goneril.

34-5. **carbonado:** slash, as meat was slashed for broiling

35. **Come your ways:** come on.

37. **neat:** dandified

43. **flesh ye:** give you your first experience of bloodshed

Osw. Why, what a monstrous fellow art thou, thus to
rail on one that's neither known of thee nor knows thee!

Kent. What a brazen-faced varlet art thou, to deny 25
thou knowest me! Is it two days ago since I tripped up
thy heels and beat thee before the King? [*Draws his
sword.*] Draw, you rogue! for, though it be night, yet
the moon shines. I'll make a sop o' the moonshine of
you. You whoreson cullionly barbermonger, draw! 30

Osw. Away! I have nothing to do with thee.

Kent. Draw, you rascal! You come with letters against
the King, and take Vanity the puppet's part against the
royalty of her father. Draw, you rogue, or I'll so carbonado your shanks! Draw, you rascal! Come your ways! 35

Osw. Help, ho! murder! help!

Kent. Strike, you slave! Stand, rogue! Stand, you neat
slave! Strike! [*Beats him.*]

Osw. Help, ho! murder! murder!

Enter *Edmund*, with his rapier drawn. 40

Edm. How now? What's the matter? *Parts* [*them*].

Kent. With you, goodman boy, if you please! Come,
I'll flesh ye! Come on, young master!

Enter *Gloucester, Cornwall, Regan, Servants.*

Glou. Weapons? arms? What's the matter here?

Corn. Keep peace, upon your lives! 45
He dies that strikes again. What is the matter?

Reg. The messengers from our sister and the King.

Corn. What is your difference? Speak.

Osw. I am scarce in breath, my lord.

51. **disclaims in thee:** denies thee

59. **At suit of:** because of

60. **zed:** the letter "z"

61. **unbolted:** unadulterated, complete

62. **jakes:** privy

71. **intrinse:** probably a combination of intrinsic and intricate

74. **Renege, affirm:** say "yes" and "no" to please the whims of their masters; **halcyon:** a seabird which it was believed would act as a weathervane if hung up

78. **Smile you:** do you smile at

79. **Goose:** flocks of geese inhabited the moors near the site associated with the legendary Camelot. **Sarum Plain:** Salisbury Plain

Kent. No marvel, you have so bestirred your valor. 50
You cowardly rascal, nature disclaims in thee; a tailor
made thee.

Corn. Thou art a strange fellow. A tailor make a man?

Kent. A tailor, sir: a stonecutter or a painter could not
have made him so ill, though they had been but two 55
hours at the trade.

Corn. Speak yet, how grew your quarrel?

Osw. This ancient ruffian, sir, whose life I have spared
At suit of his grey beard—

Kent. Thou whoreson zed! thou unnecessary letter! 60
My lord, if you'll give me leave, I will tread this unbolted
villain into mortar and daub the wall of a jakes with him.
"Spare my grey beard," you wagtail?

Corn. Peace, sirrah!
You beastly knave, know you no reverence? 65

Kent. Yes, sir, but anger hath a privilege.

Corn. Why art thou angry?

Kent. That such a slave as this should wear a sword,
Who wears no honesty. Such smiling rogues as these,
Like rats, oft bite the holy cords atwain 70
Which are too intrinse to unloose; smooth every passion
That in the natures of their lords rebel,
Being oil to fire, snow to the colder moods;
Renege, affirm, and turn their halcyon beaks
With every gale and vary of their masters, 75
Knowing naught (like dogs) but following.
A plague upon your epileptic visage!
Smile you my speeches, as I were a fool?
Goose, if I had you upon Sarum Plain,
I'd drive ye cackling home to Camelot. 80

Corn. What, art thou mad, old fellow?

Glou. How fell you out? Say that.

87. **likes me not**: does not please me

89. **plain**: straightforward in speech

94. **affect**: consciously adopt

95-6. **constrains the garb/ Quite from his nature**: plays the role so thoroughly as to distort his real nature

98. **so**: so much the better

101. **silly-ducking observants**: servants who carry obsequious bowing and scraping to extreme lengths

102. **stretch their duties nicely**: are meticulous in exerting themselves to please their masters

111-12. **though I should win your displeasure to entreat me to it**: though your displeasure at my plain speech should be an inducement to offer flattery instead

Kent. No contraries hold more antipathy
Than I and such a knave.

   Corn. Why dost thou call him knave? What is his   85
    fault?

   Kent. His countenance likes me not.

   Corn. No more perchance does mine, nor his, nor hers.

   Kent. Sir, 'tis my occupation to be plain:
I have seen better faces in my time   90
Than stands on any shoulder that I see
Before me at this instant.

   Corn.   This is some fellow
Who, having been praised for bluntness, doth affect
A saucy roughness, and constrains the garb   95
Quite from his nature. He cannot flatter, he,
An honest mind and plain, he must speak truth:
An they will take it, so; if not, he's plain.
These kind of knaves I know which in this plainness
Harbor more craft and more corrupter ends   100
Than twenty silly-ducking observants
That stretch their duties nicely.

   Kent. Sir, in good faith, in sincere verity,
Under the allowance of your great aspect,
Whose influence, like the wreath of radiant fire   105
On flickering Phœbus' front—

   Corn.   What meanest by this?

   Kent. To go out of my dialect, which you discommend
so much. I know, sir, I am no flatterer. He that beguiled
you in a plain accent was a plain knave, which, for my   110
part, I will not be, though I should win your displeasure
to entreat me to it.

   Corn. What was the offense you gave him?

   Osw. I never gave him any.

116. **upon his misconstruction:** due to his misunderstanding an action of mine

117. **compact:** acting in agreement with the King

119. **put upon him such a deal of man:** behaved so heroically

120. **worthied him:** made him appear worthy

122. **in the fleshment:** still excited from his previous encounter

125. **Ajax is their fool:** all such rogues and cowards put on a show of superiority to men who are really their superiors. Possibly a reference to the story of Troilus and Cressida in which Thersites treats Ajax as a fool.

127. **stubborn:** untamable; **reverend:** aged

132. **malice:** ill will

133. **grace:** honor due him as a King

141. **color:** kind

It pleased the King his master very late   115
To strike at me, upon his misconstruction;
When he, compact, and flattering his displeasure,
Tripped me behind; being down, insulted, railed
And put upon him such a deal of man
That worthied him, got praises of the King   120
For him attempting who was self-subdued;
And, in the fleshment of this dread exploit,
Drew on me here again.

   Kent.   None of these rogues and cowards
But Ajax is their fool.   125

   Corn.   Fetch forth the stocks!
You stubborn ancient knave, you reverend braggart,
We'll teach you—

   Kent.   Sir, I am too old to learn.
Call not your stocks for me. I serve the King,   130
On whose employment I was sent to you.
You shall do small respect, show too bold malice
Against the grace and person of my master,
Stocking his messenger.

   Corn. Fetch forth the stocks! As I have life and honor,   135
There shall he sit till noon.

   Reg. Till noon? Till night, my lord, and all night too!

   Kent. Why, madam, if I were your father's dog,
You should not use me so.

   Reg.   Sir, being his knave, I will.   140

   Corn. This is a fellow of the selfsame color
Our sister speaks of. Come, bring away the stocks!

                        Stocks brought out.

   Glou. Let me beseech your Grace not to do so.
His fault is much, and the good King his master
Will check him for it. Your purposed low correction   145
Is such as basest and contemnedest wretches

151. **answer:** take responsibility for

159. **rubbed:** hindered

166. **saw:** proverb

167-68. **out of heaven's benediction comest/ To the warm sun:** leave the shade for the discomfort of exposure to the sun. Kent comments on Lear's folly in giving away his wealth and power and leaving himself at the mercy of his daughters.

171-72. **Nothing almost sees miracles/ But misery:** nothing is closer to the miraculous than unexpected relief from one's misery.

174. **obscured course:** disguised attendance on Lear

175. **enormous:** changed from its normal order, referring to the eclipse of Lear's authority and the disordered effect of rule by two parties who disagree

176. **o'erwatched:** overexerted, since he has gone without sleep for some time

For pilferings and most common trespasses
Are punished with. The King must take it ill
That he, so slightly valued in his messenger,
Should have him thus restrained.   150
   Corn.   I'll answer that.
   Reg. My sister may receive it much more worse,
To have her gentleman abused, assaulted,
For following her affairs. Put in his legs.
                        [Kent is put in the stocks.]
Come, my good lord, away.   155
                 Exeunt [all but Gloucester and Kent].
   Glou. I am sorry for thee, friend. 'Tis the Duke's
    pleasure,
Whose disposition, all the world well knows,
Will not be rubbed nor stopped. I'll entreat for thee.
   Kent. Pray do not, sir. I have watched and travelled 160
    hard.
Some time I shall sleep out, the rest I'll whistle.
A good man's fortune may grow out at heels.
Give you good morrow!
   Glou. The Duke's to blame in this; 'twill be ill taken. 165
                              Exit.
   Kent. Good King, that must approve the common saw,
Thou out of heaven's benediction comest
To the warm sun!
Approach, thou beacon to this under globe,
That by thy comfortable beams I may   170
Peruse this letter. Nothing almost sees miracles
But misery. I know 'tis from Cordelia,
Who hath most fortunately been informed
Of my obscured course—and *[Reads]* "shall find time
From this enormous state, seeking to give   175
Losses their remedies"—All weary and o'erwatched,

177. **vantage:** advantage

179. **Fortune . . . turn thy wheel:** Fortune was emblematically pictured as a woman with a wheel to which were bound human beings. The lot of each was regulated upward or downward as the wheel was turned.

⁘⁘⁘⁘⁘⁘⁘⁘⁘⁘⁘⁘⁘⁘⁘⁘⁘⁘⁘⁘⁘⁘⁘⁘⁘⁘⁘⁘⁘⁘⁘⁘⁘⁘⁘⁘

II. [**iii.**] Edgar appears in a wood and disguises himself as a madman.

⁘⁘⁘⁘⁘⁘⁘⁘⁘⁘⁘⁘⁘⁘⁘⁘⁘⁘⁘⁘⁘⁘⁘⁘⁘⁘⁘

2. **happy:** opportune

10. **elf:** matted and tangled hair, "elf locks," was ascribed to the mischief of elves.

11. **presented:** exhibited

14. **Bedlam:** see I. ii. 132-33. A Bedlam beggar was a former inmate of Bethlehem Hospital whose senses were sufficiently recovered to permit him to beg his living.

15. **mortified:** synonymous with "numbed"

17. **object:** spectacle; **low:** humble

18. **pelting:** worthless

19. **bans:** banes, curses

20. **"Poor Turlygod! poor Tom":** Edgar quotes lines appropriate for his role as a Tom o' Bedlam. The meaning of Turlygod is obscure; possibly it is the name of a similar bedlam character which would have been familiar to Shakespeare's audience.

Take vantage, heavy eyes, not to behold
This shameful lodging.
Fortune, good night; smile once more, turn thy wheel.
Sleeps.

[Scene III. Open country in the neighborhood
of Gloucester's Castle.]

Enter *Edgar*.

Edg. I heard myself proclaimed,
And by the happy hollow of a tree
Escaped the hunt. No port is free, no place
That guard and most unusual vigilance
Does not attend my taking. Whiles I may scape,   5
I will preserve myself; and am bethought
To take the basest and most poorest shape
That ever penury, in contempt of man,
Brought near to beast. My face I'll grime with filth,
Blanket my loins, elf all my hair in knots,   10
And with presented nakedness outface
The winds and persecutions of the sky.
The country gives me proof and precedent
Of Bedlam beggars, who, with roaring voices,
Strike in their numbed and mortified bare arms   15
Pins, wooden pricks, nails, sprigs of rosemary;
And with this horrible object, from low farms,
Poor pelting villages, sheepcotes, and mills,
Sometime with lunatic bans, sometime with prayers,
Enforce their charity. "Poor Turlygod! poor Tom!"   20
That's something yet! Edgar I nothing am.   *Exit.*

II. [iv.] Lear, having found Regan absent from her castle, comes to Gloucester's castle and is enraged to find Kent in the stocks. He finds it hard to believe that Regan would so humiliate him and tells her of Goneril's mistreatment and curtailment of his followers to fifty men. Presently Goneril also arrives at Gloucester's castle and the two sisters agree that the King must dismiss all his followers. Beside himself with rage and humiliation, he departs into the stormy night.

11. **cruel:** a pun on "cruel" and "crewel" (worsted yarn, from which hose were made)

14. **over-lusty at legs:** that is, stocks are often the lot of men of vagrant habit.

14-5. **nether-stocks:** stockings

16. **so much thy place mistook:** so underestimated your dignity

[Scene IV. Without the gates of Gloucester's
Castle; Kent in the stocks.]

Enter *Lear, Fool,* and *Gentleman.*

Lear. 'Tis strange that they should so depart from
   home,
And not send back my messenger.
   Gent.   As I learned,
The night before there was no purpose in them   5
Of this remove.
   Kent.   Hail to thee, noble master!
   Lear. Ha!
Makest thou this shame thy pastime?
   Kent.   No, my lord.   10
   Fool. Ha, ha! he wears cruel garters.
Horses are tied by the head, dogs and bears by the neck,
monkeys by the loins, and men by the legs. When a
man's over-lusty at legs, then he wears wooden nether-
stocks.   15
   Lear. What's he that hath so much thy place mistook
To set thee here?
   Kent.   It is both he and she—
Your son and daughter.
   Lear. No.   20
   Kent. Yes.
   Lear. No, I say.
   Kent. I say yea.
   Lear. No, no, they would not!
   Kent. Yes, they have.   25
   Lear. By Jupiter, I swear no!

30. **To do upon respect such violent outrage:** to forget the respect due the King in mistreating his agent

31. **Resolve me:** explain to me

37. **post:** messenger

40. **spite of intermission:** although it interrupted Kent's business

41. **presently:** at once; see I. ii. 100.

42. **meinie:** company of servants and attendants

57. **bags:** moneybags

Kent. By Juno, I swear ay!

Lear.   They durst not do it;
They could not, would not do it. 'Tis worse than murder
To do upon respect such violent outrage.   30
Resolve me with all modest haste which way
Thou mightst deserve or they impose this usage,
Coming from us.

Kent.   My lord, when at their home
I did commend your Highness' letters to them,   35
Ere I was risen from the place that showed
My duty kneeling, came there a reeking post,
Stewed in his haste, half breathless, panting forth
From Goneril his mistress salutations;
Delivered letters, spite of intermission,   40
Which presently they read; on whose contents,
They summoned up their meinie, straight took horse,
Commanded me to follow and attend
The leisure of their answer, gave me cold looks,
And meeting here the other messenger,   45
Whose welcome I perceived had poisoned mine—
Being the very fellow which of late
Displayed so saucily against your Highness—
Having more man than wit about me, drew.
He raised the house with loud and coward cries.   50
Your son and daughter found this trespass worth
The shame which here it suffers.

Fool. Winter's not gone yet, if the wild geese fly that
way.

    Fathers that wear rags   55
       Do make their children blind;
    But fathers that bear bags
       Shall see their children kind.

59. **Fortune, that arrant whore:** "arrant" means notorious. Fortune was frequently described in similar terms because of her fickleness.

61. **dolors:** sorrows, with a pun on the similarity to "dollars," a Spanish coin

63, 64. **mother, Hysterica passio:** synonymous for an hysterical ailment, believed to originate in the abdominal regions, and characterized by a feeling of fullness, as of wind, which produced a choking sensation in the throat

> Fortune, that arrant whore,
>   Ne'er turns the key to the poor.   60

But for all this, thou shalt have as many dolors for thy
daughters as thou canst tell in a year.

Lear. O, how this mother swells up toward my heart!
Hysterica passio! Down, thou climbing sorrow,
Thy element's below! Where is this daughter?   65

Kent. With the Earl, sir, here within.

Lear.   Follow me not;
Stay here.   *Exit.*

Gent. Made you no more offense but what you speak
of?

Kent. None.   70
How chance the King comes with so small a number?

Fool. An thou hadst been set i' the stocks for that
question, thou'dst well deserved it.

Kent. Why, fool?

Fool. We'll set thee to school to an ant, to teach thee   75
there's no laboring i' the winter. All that follow their
noses are led by their eyes but blind men, and there's not
a nose among twenty but can smell him that's stinking.
Let go thy hold when a great wheel runs down a hill,
lest it break thy neck with following it; but the great   80
one that goes upward, let him draw thee after. When a
wise man gives thee better counsel, give me mine again:
I would have none but knaves follow it, since a fool
gives it.

> That sir which serves and seeks for gain,   85
>   And follows but for form,
> Will pack when it begins to rain
>   And leave thee in the storm.
> But I will tarry; the fool will stay,
>   And let the wise man fly.   90

91-2. **The knave turns fool that runs away;/ The fool no knave, perdy**: higher wisdom would dictate loyalty to his master; so the rogue who abandons his duty abandons wisdom as well, but the fool who will not do so is at least not a rogue.

92. **perdy**: by God, verily

97. **fetches**: fabricated excuses

98. **flying off**: a synonym for revolt

116-17. **Infirmity doth still neglect all office/ Whereto our health is bound**: sickness always produces a lapse of the attention to duty which is usual in the healthy man.

120. **am fallen out with my more headier will**: regret my first impulsiveness

    The knave turns fool that runs away;
        The fool no knave, perdy.
Kent. Where learned you this, fool?
Fool. Not i' the stocks, fool.

        Enter *Lear* and *Gloucester.*

  Lear. Deny to speak with me? They are sick! they are   95
    weary!
They have travelled all the night! Mere fetches—
The images of revolt and flying off!
Fetch me a better answer.
  Glou.   My dear lord,   100
You know the fiery quality of the Duke,
How unremovable and fixed he is
In his own course.
  Lear. Vengeance! plague! death! confusion!
Fiery? What quality? Why, Gloucester, Gloucester,   105
I'd speak with the Duke of Cornwall and his wife.
  Glou. Well, my good lord, I have informed them so.
  Lear. Informed them? Dost thou understand me, man?
  Glou. Ay, my good lord.
  Lear. The King would speak with Cornwall; the dear   110
    father
Would with his daughter speak, commands, tends service.
Are they informed of this? My breath and blood!
Fiery? the fiery Duke? Tell the hot Duke that—
No, but not yet! May be he is not well.   115
Infirmity doth still neglect all office
Whereto our health is bound. We are not ourselves
When nature, being oppressed, commands the mind
To suffer with the body. I'll forbear;
And am fallen out with my more headier will,   120

126. **Give me my servant forth**: that is, release Kent from the stocks.

133. **cockney**: this word had various meanings, but here seems to indicate a cook too simple-minded to know she should kill her eels before attempting to bake them in a pie.

134. **paste**: pastry for a meat pie; **knapped**: rapped

143-44. **I would divorce me from thy mother's tomb,/ Sepulchring an adultress**: I would refuse to be buried in my wife's tomb because she had produced a daughter not of my begetting.

146. **naught**: wicked

146-47. **she hath tied/ Sharp-toothed unkindness, like a vulture, here**: a reference to the torture of Prometheus, who was bound while vultures gnawed at his vitals as a punishment for his transmittal of fire to men

To take the indisposed and sickly fit
For the sound man. [*Looks at Kent.*] Death on my state!
    Wherefore
Should he sit here? This act persuades me
That this remotion of the Duke and her   125
Is practice only. Give me my servant forth.
Go tell the Duke and's wife I'd speak with them—
Now, presently. Bid them come forth and hear me,
Or at their chamber door I'll beat the drum
Till it cry sleep to death.   130
   Glou. I would have all well betwixt you.   *Exit.*
   Lear. O me, my heart, my rising heart! But down!
   Fool. Cry to it, nuncle, as the cockney did to the eels
when she put 'em i' the paste alive. She knapped 'em o'
the coxcombs with a stick and cried "Down, wantons,   135
down!" 'Twas her brother that, in pure kindness to his
horse, buttered his hay.

Enter *Cornwall, Regan, Gloucester, Servants.*

   Lear. Good morrow to you both.
   Corn.   Hail to your Grace!
                    Kent here set at liberty.
   Reg. I am glad to see your Highness.   140
   Lear. Regan, I think you are; I know what reason
I have to think so. If thou shouldst not be glad,
I would divorce me from thy mother's tomb,
Sepulchring an adultress. [*To Kent*] O, are you free?
Some other time for that.—Beloved Regan,   145
Thy sister's naught. O Regan, she hath tied
Sharp-toothed unkindness, like a vulture, here!
                     [*Points to his heart.*]

161-62. **Nature in you stands on the very verge/Of her confine**: your term of life is nearing its end.

163. **some discretion**: outside himself, i.e., some other more discreet person

180. **taking**: infectious

I can scarce speak to thee. Thou'lt not believe
With how depraved a quality—O Regan!

   Reg. I pray you, sir, take patience. I have hope   150
You less know how to value her desert
Than she to scant her duty.

   Lear.   Say, how is that?

   Reg. I cannot think my sister in the least
Would fail her obligation. If, sir, perchance   155
She have restrained the riots of your followers,
'Tis on such ground, and to such wholesome end,
As clears her from all blame.

   Lear. My curses on her!

   Reg.   O, sir, you are old!   160
Nature in you stands on the very verge
Of her confine. You should be ruled, and led
By some discretion that discerns your state
Better than you yourself. Therefore I pray you
That to our sister you do make return;   165
Say you have wronged her.

   Lear.   Ask her forgiveness?
Do you but mark how this becomes the house:
[*Kneeling*] "Dear daughter, I confess that I am old.
Age is unnecessary. On my knees I beg   170
That you'll vouchsafe me raiment, bed, and food."

   Reg. Good sir, no more! These are unsightly tricks.
Return you to my sister.

   Lear.   [*Stands up.*] Never, Regan!
She hath abated me of half my train;   175
Looked black upon me; struck me with her tongue,
Most serpent-like, upon the very heart.
All the stored vengeances of heaven fall
On her ingrateful top! Strike her young bones,
You taking airs, with lameness!   180

189. **tender-hefted:** too tender, or too susceptible to tenderness, to behave cruelly

193. **scant my sizes:** give me scanty allowances

194-95. **oppose the bolt/ Against my coming in:** refuse me admission

197. **effects of courtesy:** courteous behavior

203. **approves:** proves; see I. i. 201.

Corn.   Fie, sir, fie!

Lear. You nimble lightnings, dart your blinding flames
Into her scornful eyes! Infect her beauty,
You fen-sucked fogs, drawn by the powerful sun,
To fall and blister!   185

Reg. O the blest gods! so will you wish on me
When the rash mood is on.

Lear. No, Regan, thou shalt never have my curse.
Thy tender-hefted nature shall not give
Thee o'er to harshness. Her eyes are fierce, but thine   190
Do comfort and not burn. 'Tis not in thee
To grudge my pleasures, to cut off my train,
To bandy hasty words, to scant my sizes,
And, in conclusion, to oppose the bolt
Against my coming in. Thou better knowest   195
The offices of nature, bond of childhood,
Effects of courtesy, dues of gratitude.
Thy half of the kingdom hast thou not forgot,
Wherein I thee endowed.

Reg.   Good sir, to the purpose.   200

Lear. Who put my man in the stocks?   *Tucket within.*

Corn.   What trumpet's that?

Reg. I know it—my sister's. This approves her letter
That she would soon be here.

Enter [*Oswald* the] *Steward.*

                          Is your lady come?   205

Lear. This is a slave, whose easy, borrowed pride
Dwells in the fickle grace of her he follows.
Out, varlet, from my sight!

Corn.   What means your Grace?

224. **disorders**: misbehavior
234. **abjure**: renounce

Lear. Who stocked my servant? Regan, I have good   210
   hope
Thou didst not know on't.

Enter *Goneril.*

                 Who comes here? O heavens,
If you do love old men, if your sweet sway
Allow obedience, if you yourselves are old,   215
Make it your cause! Send down, and take my part!
[*To Goneril*] Art not ashamed to look upon this beard?—
O Regan, will you take her by the hand?
   Gon. Why not by the hand, sir? How have I offended?
All's not offense that indiscretion finds   220
And dotage terms so.
   Lear.   O sides, you are too tough!
Will you yet hold? How came my man i' the stocks?
   Corn. I set him there, sir, but his own disorders
Deserved much less advancement.   225
   Lear.   You? Did you?
   Reg. I pray you, father, being weak, seem so.
If, till the expiration of your month,
You will return and sojourn with my sister,
Dismissing half your train, come then to me.   230
I am now from home, and out of that provision
Which shall be needful for your entertainment.
   Lear. Return to her, and fifty men dismissed?
No, rather I abjure all roofs, and choose
To wage against the enmity o' the air,   235
To be a comrade with the wolf and owl—
Necessity's sharp pinch! Return with her?
Why, the hot-blooded France, that dowerless took
Our youngest born, I could as well be brought

242. **sumpter:** pack animal
254. **Thunder-bearer:** Jove
268. **sith that:** since

To knee his throne, and, squire-like, pension beg   240
To keep base life afoot. Return with her?
Persuade me rather to be slave and sumpter
To this detested groom.   [*Pointing at Oswald.*]
  Gon.   At your choice, sir.
  Lear. I prithee, daughter, do not make me mad.   245
I will not trouble thee, my child; farewell.
We'll no more meet, no more see one another.
But yet thou art my flesh, my blood, my daughter;
Or rather a disease that's in my flesh,
Which I must needs call mine. Thou art a boil,   250
A plague sore or embossed carbuncle,
In my corrupted blood. But I'll not chide thee.
Let shame come when it will, I do not call it.
I do not bid the Thunder-bearer shoot,
Nor tell tales of thee to high-judging Jove.   255
Mend when thou canst; be better at thy leisure;
I can be patient; I can stay with Regan,
I and my hundred knights.
  Reg.   Not altogether so.
I looked not for you yet, nor am provided   260
For your fit welcome. Give ear, sir, to my sister;
For those that mingle reason with your passion
Must be content to think you old, and so—
But she knows what she does.
  Lear.   Is this well spoken?   265
  Reg. I dare avouch it, sir. What, fifty followers?
Is it not well? What should you need of more?
Yea, or so many, sith that both charge and danger
Speak 'gainst so great a number? How in one house
Should many people, under two commands,   270
Hold amity? 'Tis hard; almost impossible.

274. **slack:** neglect

287-89. **Those wicked creatures yet do look well-favored/ When others are more wicked; not being the worst/ Stands in some rank of praise:** wickedness has degrees and wicked persons seem nearer to virtue when compared with others of greater wickedness.

298-99. **Our basest beggars/ Are in the poorest thing superfluous:** even beggars have more than they need.

302-4. **If only to go warm were gorgeous,/ Why, nature needs not what thou gorgeous wearest,/ Which scarcely keeps thee warm:** your dress has decorative additions which do not add to the warmth it provides.

Gon. Why might not you, my lord, receive attendance
From those that she calls servants, or from mine?
    Reg. Why not, my lord? If then they chanced to slack
      ye,   275
We could control them. If you will come to me
(For now I spy a danger), I entreat you
To bring but five-and-twenty. To no more
Will I give place or notice.
    Lear. I gave you all—   280
    Reg.   And in good time you gave it!
    Lear. Made you my guardians, my depositaries;
But kept a reservation to be followed
With such a number. What, must I come to you
With five-and-twenty, Regan? Said you so?   285
    Reg. And speak it again, my lord. No more with me.
    Lear. Those wicked creatures yet do look well-favored
When others are more wicked; not being the worst
Stands in some rank of praise. [*To Goneril*] I'll go with
      thee.   290
Thy fifty yet doth double five-and-twenty,
And thou art twice her love.
    Gon.   Hear me, my lord.
What need you five-and-twenty, ten, or five,
To follow in a house where twice so many   295
Have a command to tend you?
    Reg.   What need one?
    Lear. O, reason not the need! Our basest beggars
Are in the poorest thing superfluous.
Allow not nature more than nature needs,   300
Man's life is cheap as beast's. Thou art a lady:
If only to go warm were gorgeous,
Why, nature needs not what thou gorgeous wearest,
Which scarcely keeps thee warm. But, for true need—

309. **fool me not so much:** do not make me such a weakling.

319. **flaws:** fragments, though probably several meanings are suggested here. A flaw also meant "a short burst of passion," and "a squall of rain and wind." The Folio text has a stage direction just above this line, "Storm and Tempest."

323. **bestowed:** accommodated

326. **his particular:** his own person

You heavens, give me that patience, patience I need!   305
You see me here, you gods, a poor old man,
As full of grief as age; wretched in both.
If it be you that stirs these daughters' hearts
Against their father, fool me not so much
To bear it tamely; touch me with noble anger,   310
And let not women's weapons, water drops,
Stain my man's cheeks! No, you unnatural hags!
I will have such revenges on you both
That all the world shall—I will do such things—
What they are yet, I know not; but they shall be   315
The terrors of the earth! You think I'll weep.
No, I'll not weep.   [*Sounds of an approaching storm.*]
I have full cause of weeping, but this heart
Shall break into a hundred thousand flaws
Or ere I'll weep. O fool, I shall go mad!   320
    Exeunt Lear, Gloucester, Kent, and Fool.
 Corn. Let us withdraw, 'twill be a storm.
 Reg. This house is little; the old man and's people
Cannot be well bestowed.
 Gon. 'Tis his own blame; hath put himself from rest
And must needs taste his folly.   325
 Reg. For his particular, I'll receive him gladly,
But not one follower.
 Gon.   So am I purposed.
Where is my Lord of Gloucester?
 Corn. Followed the old man forth.   330

Enter *Gloucester*.

      He is returned.
 Glou. The King is in high rage.
 Corn.   Whither is he going?

338. **sorely ruffle:** grievously rage
345. **have his ear abused:** listen to reckless talk

Glou. He calls to horse, but will I know not whither.

Corn. 'Tis best to give him way, he leads himself.   335

Gon. My lord, entreat him by no means to stay.

Glou. Alack, the night comes on, and the bleak winds
Do sorely ruffle. For many miles about
There's scarce a bush.

Reg.   O, sir, to wilful men   340
The injuries that they themselves procure
Must be their schoolmasters. Shut up your doors.
He is attended with a desperate train,
And what they may incense him to, being apt
To have his ear abused, wisdom bids fear.   345

Corn. Shut up your doors, my lord; 'tis a wild night.
My Regan counsels well. Come out o' the storm.

                        [*Exeunt.*]

KING LEAR

ACT III

III. i. On the storm-whipped heath, Kent encounters one of Lear's men, who describes the King buffeted by the storm. Kent informs him that a secret strife is brewing between the forces of Albany and Cornwall and that the King of France and Cordelia are sending forces to rescue Lear. Kent sends the man to Dover to convey messages to Cordelia.

|||||||||||||||||||||||||||||||||||||

9. **make nothing of:** treat with no respect
12. **cub-drawn:** sucked dry by her young
13. **belly-pinched:** hungry
20. **dare upon the warrant of my note:** gamble on my knowledge of you
21. **dear:** important

ACT III

Scene I. [A heath.]

Storm still. Enter *Kent* and a *Gentleman,* severally.

Kent. Who's there, besides foul weather?
Gent. One minded like the weather, most unquietly.
Kent. I know you. Where's the King?
Gent. Contending with the fretful elements;
Bids the wind blow the earth into the sea,   5
Or swell the curled waters 'bove the main,
That things might change or cease; tears his white hair,
Which the impetuous blasts, with eyeless rage,
Catch in their fury and make nothing of;
Strives in his little world of man to outscorn   10
The to-and-fro-conflicting wind and rain.
This night, wherein the cub-drawn bear would couch,
The lion and the belly-pinched wolf
Keep their fur dry, unbonneted he runs,
And bids what will take all.   15
    Kent.   But who is with him?
    Gent. None but the fool, who labors to outjest
His heart-struck injuries.
    Kent.   Sir, I do know you,
And dare upon the warrant of my note   20
Commend a dear thing to you. There is division

58

24-5. **as who have not, that their great stars/ Throned and set high:** that is, as have all those who have been advanced by fortune to high positions of authority

26. **speculations:** synonymous with "spies"

28. **snuffs:** hasty quarrels; **packings:** plottings

31. **furnishings:** pretexts

35. **at point:** on the point of

41. **plain:** complain

48. **my out-wall:** my outward appearance

51. **that fellow:** myself

(Although as yet the face of it is covered
With mutual cunning) 'twixt Albany and Cornwall;
Who have (as who have not, that their great stars
Throned and set high?) servants, who seem no less,   25
Which are to France the spies and speculations
Intelligent of our state. What hath been seen,
Either in snuffs and packings of the Dukes,
Or the hard rein which both of them have borne
Against the old kind King, or something deeper,   30
Whereof, perchance, these are but furnishings—
But, true it is, from France there comes a power
Into this scattered kingdom, who already,
Wise in our negligence, have secret feet
In some of our best ports and are at point   35
To show their open banner. Now to you:
If on my credit you dare build so far
To make your speed to Dover, you shall find
Some that will thank you, making just report
Of how unnatural and bemadding sorrow   40
The King hath cause to plain.
I am a gentleman of blood and breeding,
And from some knowledge and assurance offer
This office to you.
    Gent. I will talk further with you.   45
    Kent.   No, do not.
For confirmation that I am much more
Than my out-wall, open this purse and take
What it contains. If you shall see Cordelia
(As fear not but you shall), show her this ring,   50
And she will tell you who that fellow is
That yet you do not know. Fie on this storm!
I will go seek the King.
    Gent. Give me your hand. Have you no more to say?

56-7. in which your pain/ That way, I'll this: you search that way and I will search this way.

⠿⠿⠿⠿⠿⠿⠿⠿⠿⠿⠿⠿⠿⠿⠿⠿⠿⠿⠿⠿⠿⠿⠿⠿⠿⠿⠿⠿⠿⠿⠿⠿⠿⠿⠿⠿

III. ii. In another part of the heath, Lear, with only the Fool for his companion, rages against the terrors of the storm. There Kent finds him and guides him to a hovel.

⠿⠿⠿⠿⠿⠿⠿⠿⠿⠿⠿⠿⠿⠿⠿⠿⠿⠿⠿⠿⠿⠿⠿⠿⠿⠿⠿

2. **cataracts and hurricanoes:** both names for whirl-pools

3. **cocks:** weathercocks

5. **Vaunt-couriers:** heralds

8. **germens:** human germs, sperm

10. **court holy water:** flattery

18. **subscription:** allegiance

Kent. Few words, but, to effect, more than all yet: 55
That, when we have found the King (in which your pain
That way, I'll this), he that first lights on him
Holla the other.

Exeunt [severally].

Scene II. [Another part of the heath.]

Storm still. Enter *Lear* and *Fool.*

Lear. Blow, winds, and crack your cheeks! rage! blow!
You cataracts and hurricanoes, spout
Till you have drenched our steeples, drowned the cocks!
You sulph'rous and thought-executing fires,
Vaunt-couriers of oak-cleaving thunderbolts, 5
Singe my white head! And thou, all-shaking thunder,
Strike flat the thick rotundity o' the world,
Crack Nature's molds, all germens spill at once,
That make ingrateful man!

Fool. O nuncle, court holy water in a dry house is bet- 10
ter than this rain water out o' door. Good nuncle, in; ask
thy daughters' blessing! Here's a night pities neither wise
men nor fools.

Lear. Rumble thy bellyful! Spit, fire! Spout, rain!
Nor rain, wind, thunder, fire are my daughters. 15
I tax not you, you elements, with unkindness.
I never gave you kingdom, called you children,
You owe me no subscription. Then let fall
Your horrible pleasure. Here I stand your slave,
A poor, infirm, weak, and despised old man. 20

23. **high-engendered**: originating in the heavens

27. **codpiece**: an appendage to the front of male hose or breeches to cover the genitals, here used for the genitals themselves

27-30. **The codpiece . . . many**: the man who hastily begets children when he has no roof over his head will become a verminous vagrant.

31-4. **The man . . . wake**: the man whose sense of values is so poor as to cherish a meaner member as much as his heart will correspondingly suffer unduly from trivial woes.

44. **Gallow**: terrify

But yet I call you servile ministers,
That will with two pernicious daughters join
Your high-engendered battles 'gainst a head
So old and white as this! O, ho! 'tis foul!

   Fool. He that has a house to put's head in has a good   25
headpiece.

         The codpiece that will house
           Before the head has any,
         The head and he shall louse:
           So beggars marry many.   30
         The man that makes his toe
           What he his heart should make
         Shall of a corn cry woe,
           And turn his sleep to wake.

For there was never yet fair woman but she made mouths   35
in a glass.

Enter Kent.

   Lear. No, I will be the pattern of all patience;
I will say nothing.

   Kent. Who's there?

   Fool. Marry, here's grace and a codpiece; that's a wise   40
man and a fool.

   Kent. Alas, sir, are you here? Things that love night
Love not such nights as these. The wrathful skies
Gallow the very wanderers of the dark
And make them keep their caves. Since I was man,   45
Such sheets of fire, such bursts of horrid thunder,
Such groans of roaring wind and rain, I never
Remember to have heard. Man's nature cannot carry
The affliction nor the fear.

   Lear.   Let the great gods,   50

51. **pudder:** pother, disturbance

55. **simular:** simulator

56. **Caitiff:** a base person both wicked and miserable

57. **under covert and convenient seeming:** by hypocrisy

59. **Rive:** split

59-60. **cry/ These dreadful summoners grace:** beg mercy of the threatening elements.

63. **hard by:** near by

That keep this dreadful pudder o'er our heads,
Find out their enemies now. Tremble, thou wretch,
That hast within thee undivulged crimes
Unwhipped of justice. Hide thee, thou bloody hand;
Thou perjured, and thou simular of virtue   55
That art incestuous. Caitiff, to pieces shake
That under covert and convenient seeming
Hast practiced on man's life. Close pent-up guilts,
Rive your concealing continents, and cry
These dreadful summoners grace. I am a man   60
More sinned against than sinning.
     Kent.   Alack, bareheaded?
Gracious my lord, hard by here is a hovel;
Some friendship will it lend you 'gainst the tempest.
Repose you there, while I to this hard house   65
(More harder than the stones whereof 'tis raised,
Which even but now, demanding after you,
Denied me to come in) return, and force
Their scanted courtesy.
     Lear.   My wits begin to turn.   70
Come on, my boy. How dost, my boy? Art cold?
I am cold myself. Where is this straw, my fellow?
The art of our necessities is strange,
And can make vile things precious. Come, your hovel.
Poor fool and knave, I have one part in my heart   75
That's sorry yet for thee.
     Fool. [*Sings*]
          He that has and a little tiny wit,
               With hey, ho, the wind and the rain,
          Must make content with his fortunes fit,
               Though the rain it raineth every day.   80
     Lear. True, boy. Come, bring us to this hovel.
                         Exeunt [*Lear and Kent*].

82. **brave:** splendid

84-97. **When . . . feet:** a parody of a set of verses known as "Merlin's Prophecy," at one time erroneously attributed to Chaucer. These lines are in the Folio but not the Quarto edition of *King Lear* and some scholars consider them a theatrical addition.

91. **cutpurses:** pickpockets

92. **usurers:** moneylenders

94. **Albion:** an ancient name for Britain, mainly poetic

<hr />

III. iii. Gloucester reveals to Edmund the receipt of a letter telling of the French expedition to avenge Lear, information which Edmund resolves to impart at once to the Duke of Cornwall.

Fool. This is a brave night to cool a courtesan. I'll
speak a prophecy ere I go:

When priests are more in word than matter;
When brewers mar their malt with water;   85
When nobles are their tailors' tutors,
No heretics burned, but wenches' suitors;
When every case in law is right;
No squire in debt nor no poor knight;
When slanders do not live in tongues;   90
Nor cutpurses come not to throngs;
When usurers tell their gold i' the field;
And bawds and whores do churches build:
Then shall the realm of Albion
Come to great confusion.   95
Then comes the time, who lives to see't,
That going shall be used with feet.

This prophecy Merlin shall make, for I live before his
time.   *Exit.*

Scene III. [Inside Gloucester's Castle.]

Enter *Gloucester* and *Edmund.*

Glou. Alack, alack, Edmund, I like not this unnatural
dealing! When I desired their leave that I might pity
him, they took from me the use of mine own house;
charged me on pain of perpetual displeasure neither to
speak of him, entreat for him, nor any way sustain him.   5

Edm. Most savage and unnatural!

Glou. Go to; say you nothing. There is division between the Dukes, and a worse matter than that. I have

12. **home:** with complete finality

12-3. **there is part of a power already footed:** that is, some French forces have already landed.

14. **look:** look for; **privily:** secretly

22. **fair deserving:** an action which will impress the Duke with my good will toward him

    ▬▬▬▬▬▬▬▬▬▬▬▬▬▬▬▬

III. iv. Lear and his Fool discover Edgar, still pretending to be a madman, in the hovel. Gloucester comes in search of Lear and conducts all of them back toward his castle.

    ▬▬▬▬▬▬▬▬▬▬

received a letter this night—'tis dangerous to be spoken—I 10
have locked the letter in my closet. These injuries the
King now bears will be revenged home; there is part of a
power already footed; we must incline to the King. I
will look him and privily relieve him. Go you and maintain talk with the Duke, that my charity be not of him 15
perceived. If he ask for me, I am ill and gone to bed.
If I die for it, as no less is threatened me, the King my
old master must be relieved. There are strange things
toward, Edmund. Pray you be careful. *Exit.*

Edm. This courtesy, forbid thee, shall the Duke 20
Instantly know, and of that letter too.
This seems a fair deserving, and must draw me
That which my father loses—no less than all.
The younger rises when the old doth fall. *Exit.*

Scene IV. [Before a hovel on the heath.]

Storm still. Enter *Lear, Kent,* and *Fool.*

Kent. Here is the place, my lord. Good my lord, enter.
The tyranny of the open night's too rough
For nature to endure.
  Lear.   Let me alone.
Kent. Good my lord, enter here. 5
  Lear.   Wilt break my heart?
Kent. I had rather break mine own. Good my lord,
  enter.
Lear. Thou thinkest 'tis much that this contentious
  storm 10

36. **bide:** endure

38. **looped and windowed:** full of gaping holes

39-40. **I have ta'en/ Too little care of this:** I have concerned myself too little with these facts.

42. **superflux:** the excess of your own needs

Invades us to the skin. So 'tis to thee;
But where the greater malady is fixed,
The lesser is scarce felt. Thou'dst shun a bear;
But if thy flight lay toward the roaring sea,
Thou'dst meet the bear i' the mouth. When the mind's   15
    free,
The body's delicate. The tempest in my mind
Doth from my senses take all feeling else
Save what beats there. Filial ingratitude!
Is it not as this mouth should tear this hand   20
For lifting food to it? But I will punish home!
No, I will weep no more. In such a night
To shut me out! Pour on; I will endure.
In such a night as this! O Regan, Goneril!
Your old kind father, whose frank heart gave all!   25
O, that way madness lies; let me shun that!
No more of that.

  Kent.   Good my lord, enter here.

  Lear. Prithee go in thyself; seek thine own ease.   30
This tempest will not give me leave to ponder
On things would hurt me more. But I'll go in.
[*To the Fool*] In, boy; go first.—You houseless poverty—
Nay, get thee in. I'll pray, and then I'll sleep.

       [*The Fool enters the hovel.*]

Poor naked wretches, wheresoe'er you are,   35
That bide the pelting of this pitiless storm,
How shall your houseless heads and unfed sides,
Your looped and windowed raggedness, defend you
From seasons such as these? O, I have ta'en
Too little care of this! Take physic, pomp;   40
Expose thyself to feel what wretches feel,
That thou may'st shake the superflux to them
And show the heavens more just.

44. **Fathom and half**: the rain is so heavy that Edgar apes a sailor taking soundings of the depth of water.

59-60. **that hath laid knives under his pillow and halters in his pew**: it was believed that demons often tempted men to suicide.

63. **course**: pursue; **five wits**: enumerated in Stephen Hawes, *The Pastime of Pleasure* (1509), as common wit, imagination, fantasy, estimation, and memory

64. **do de, do de**: an imitation of the chattering of teeth

65. **taking**: infection; see II. iv. 180.

66-7. **There . . . there**: Edgar snatches at different parts of his body as though to catch the demon tormenting him.

Edg. [*Within*] Fathom and half, fathom and half! Poor
Tom!   45

[Re-] Enter *Fool*.

Fool. Come not in here, nuncle, here's a spirit. Help
me, help me!
Kent. Give me thy hand. Who's there?
Fool. A spirit, a spirit! He says his name's poor Tom.
Kent. What art thou that dost grumble there i' the   50
straw? Come forth.

Enter *Edgar*.

Edg. Away! the foul fiend follows me! Through the
sharp hawthorn blow the winds. Humh! go to thy bed,
and warm thee.
Lear. Didst thou give all to thy two daughters. And   55
art thou come to this?
Edg. Who gives anything to poor Tom? whom the
foul fiend hath led through fire and through flame,
through ford and whirlpool, o'er bog and quagmire; that
hath laid knives under his pillow and halters in his pew,   60
set ratsbane by his porridge, made him proud of heart,
to ride on a bay trotting horse over four-inched bridges,
to course his own shadow for a traitor. Bless thy five wits!
Tom's acold. O, do de, do de, do de. Bless thee from
whirlwinds, star-blasting, and taking! Do poor Tom   65
some charity, whom the foul fiend vexes. There could I
have him now, and there, and there again, and there!
                                                                        Storm still.
Lear. Have his daughters brought him to this pass?
Couldst thou save nothing? Wouldst thou give 'em all?

81. **pelican daughters**: various writers of the period described the pelican as nourishing its offspring with its own blood.

82. **Pillicock**: a term of affection with facetious overtones, sometimes used to denote the phallus

82-3. **Alow, alow, loo, loo**: a kind of hunting call

100-1. **Let not the creaking of shoes nor the rustling of silks betray thy poor heart to woman**: it was fashionable to wear creaking shoes: "Do not be beguiled by women's fashionable dress."

102. **placket**: an opening in a woman's petticoat; also, a loose woman

Fool. Nay, he reserved a blanket, else we had been all   70
shamed.

Lear. Now all the plagues that in the pendulous air
Hang fated o'er men's faults light on thy daughters!

Kent. He hath no daughters, sir.

Lear. Death, traitor! Nothing could have subdued   75
nature
To such a lowness but his unkind daughters.
Is it the fashion that discarded fathers
Should have thus little mercy on their flesh?
Judicious punishment! 'Twas this flesh begot   80
Those pelican daughters.

Edg. Pillicock sat on Pillicock Hill. Alow, alow, loo,
loo!

Fool. This cold night will turn us all to fools and madmen.   85

Edg. Take heed o' the foul fiend; obey thy parents;
keep thy word's justice; swear not; commit not with
man's sworn spouse; set not thy sweet heart on proud
array. Tom's acold.

Lear. What hast thou been?   90

Edg. A servingman, proud in heart and mind; that
curled my hair, wore gloves in my cap; served the lust of
my mistress' heart and did the act of darkness with her;
swore as many oaths as I spake words, and broke them in
the sweet face of heaven; one that slept in the contriving   95
of lust, and waked to do it. Wine loved I deeply, dice
dearly; and in woman out-paramoured the Turk. False of
heart, light of ear, bloody of hand; hog in sloth, fox in
stealth, wolf in greediness, dog in madness, lion in prey.
Let not the creaking of shoes nor the rustling of silks be-   100
tray thy poor heart to woman. Keep thy foot out of
brothels, thy hand out of plackets, thy pen from lend-

104-5. **suum, . . . let him trot by:** much of Edgar's mad talk, incorporating catchwords and snatches of contemporary songs, cannot now be satisfactorily interpreted. Here he seems to be quoting several songs which have not been identified. One scholar has found a reference to "Dolphin, prince of the dead" in the Newcastle Play of Noah, and this presumably evil spirit may be the Dolphin referred to, though "Dolphin" was also the contemporary form of "Dauphin," the heir to the French throne. "Sessa," spelled "sesey" in the Folio, is thought to derive from the French *cessez,* "cease," but its exact meaning and derivation are uncertain. See III. vi. 75, and Lear's hunting cry, "Sa, sa," IV. vi. 219.

110-11. **cat:** civet cat; **Here's three on's are sophisticated:** that is, Kent, the Fool, and himself, all being fully clothed

111. **unaccommodated man:** man in his natural state without clothing

114. **naughty:** wicked; see II. iv. 146.

118. **Flibbertigibbet:** this and the other names of fiends to which Edgar refers are probably derived from Samuel Harsnett, *A Declaration of Egregious Popish Impostures* (1603), an anti-Catholic work which described and ridiculed current beliefs about demonic possession.

119-20. **the web and the pin:** a growth or film over the eye, a kind of cataract

122-26. **Swithold . . . thee:** a charm to avert the nightmare; a demon who, with her nine young, was

er's books, and defy the foul fiend. Still through the hawthorn blows the cold wind; says suum, mun, hey, no,
nonny. Dolphin my boy, my boy, sessa! let him trot by. 105
Storm still.

Lear. Thou wert better in thy grave than to answer
with thy uncovered body this extremity of the skies. Is
man no more than this? Consider him well. Thou owest
the worm no silk, the beast no hide, the sheep no wool,
the cat no perfume. Ha! Here's three on's are sophisti- 110
cated! Thou art the thing itself; unaccommodated man
is no more but such a poor, bare, forked animal as thou
art. Off, off, you lendings! Come, unbutton here.

[*Tearing his garments.*]

Fool. Prithee, nuncle, be contented! 'Tis a naughty
night to swim in. Now a little fire in a wild field were 115
like an old lecher's heart—a small spark, all the rest on's
body cold. Look, here comes a walking fire.

Enter *Gloucester* with a torch.

Edg. This is the foul Flibbertigibbet. He begins at cur-
few, and walks till the first cock. He gives the web and
the pin, squints the eye, and makes the harelip; mildews 120
the white wheat, and hurts the poor creature of earth.
Swithold footed thrice the 'old;
He met the nightmare, and her nine fold;
Bid her alight
And her troth plight, 125
And aroint thee, witch, aroint thee!

Kent. How fares your Grace?
Lear. What's he?
Kent. Who's there? What is't you seek?

supposed to ride humans and torment them while asleep. "Mare" does not mean a female horse but derives from the Anglo-Saxon word for "incubus." **'old:** wold, an upland plain; **aroint thee:** be off with you.

132. **water:** water-newt

134. **sallets:** salad greens

136. **tithing:** district of rural communities, probably a parish

148. **cannot suffer:** will not permit me

Glou. What are you there? Your names?   130
  Edg. Poor Tom, that eats the swimming frog, the toad,
the todpole, the wall-newt and the water; that in the fury
of his heart, when the foul fiend rages, eats cow-dung for
sallets, swallows the old rat and the ditch-dog, drinks the
green mantle of the standing pool; who is whipped from 135
tithing to tithing, and stock-punished and imprisoned;
who hath had three suits to his back, six shirts to his
body, horse to ride, and weapon to wear;
           But mice and rats, and such small deer,
           Have been Tom's food for seven long year.   140
Beware my follower. Peace, Smulkin! peace, thou fiend!
  Glou. What, hath your Grace no better company?
  Edg. The prince of darkness is a gentleman!
Modo he's called, and Mahu.
  Glou. Our flesh and blood, my lord, is grown so vile, 145
That it doth hate what gets it.
  Edg. Poor Tom's acold.
  Glou. Go in with me. My duty cannot suffer
T' obey in all your daughters' hard commands.
Though their injunction be to bar my doors   150
And let this tyrannous night take hold upon you,
Yet have I ventured to come seek you out
And bring you where both fire and food is ready.
  Lear. First let me talk with this philosopher.
What is the cause of thunder?   155
  Kent. Good my lord, take his offer; go into the house.
  Lear. I'll talk a word with this same learned Theban.
What is your study?
  Edg. How to prevent the fiend and to kill vermin.
  Lear. Let me ask you one word in private.   160
  Kent. Importune him once more to go, my lord.
His wits begin to unsettle.

173. **cry you mercy**: I beg your pardon.

181. **keep still**: still remain

188. **Child Rowland to the dark tower came**: possibly from a song, not identified. "Child" was the term given to a candidate for knighthood.

189. **word**: motto

190. **Fie, foh, and fum**: almost identical with the Giant's catch phrase in "Jack and the Giant Killer"

Glou. Canst thou blame him?
Storm still.

His daughters seek his death. Ah, that good Kent!
He said it would be thus—poor banished man! 165
Thou sayest the King grows mad: I'll tell thee, friend,
I am almost mad myself. I had a son,
Now outlawed from my blood. He sought my life
But lately, very late. I loved him, friend—
No father his son dearer. True to tell thee, 170
The grief hath crazed my wits. What a night's this!
I do beseech your Grace—
Lear. O, cry you mercy, sir.
Noble philosopher, your company.
Edg. Tom's acold. 175
Glou. In, fellow, there, into the hovel; keep thee
warm.
Lear. Come, let's in all.
Kent. This way, my lord.
Lear. With him! 180
I will keep still with my philosopher.
Kent. Good my lord, soothe him; let him take the
fellow.
Glou. Take him you on.
Kent. Sirrah, come on; go along with us. 185
Lear. Come, good Athenian.
Glou. No words, no words! hush.
Edg. Child Rowland to the dark tower came;
His word was still
Fie, foh, and fum! 190
I smell the blood of a British man.
Exeunt.

III. v. Cornwall receives from Edmund information that Gloucester is in league with France against him and vows soon to avenge himself and make Edmund Earl of Gloucester.

||||||||||||||||||||||||||||||||||||

3. **something fears me to think of:** gives me some concern

6. **provoking merit:** that is, Gloucester's own wickedness was an incitement to Edgar's evil.

9. **to be:** being

10. **intelligent party:** an informer

18. **comforting:** behaving as the ally of, the legal sense of the word, not merely "succoring"

19. **stuff his suspicion more fully:** add more substance to his suspicion

Scene V. [Inside Gloucester's Castle.]

Enter *Cornwall* and *Edmund*.

Corn. I will have my revenge ere I depart his house.

Edm. How, my lord, I may be censured, that nature thus gives way to loyalty, something fears me to think of.

Corn. I now perceive it was not altogether your brother's evil disposition made him seek his death; but a 5 provoking merit, set a-work by a reprovable badness in himself.

Edm. How malicious is my fortune that I must repent to be just! This is the letter he spoke of, which approves him an intelligent party to the advantages of France. O 10 heavens! that this treason were not, or not I the detector!

Corn. Go with me to the Duchess.

Edm. If the matter of this paper be certain, you have mighty business in hand.

Corn. True or false, it hath made thee Earl of Glouces- 15 ter. Seek out where thy father is, that he may be ready for our apprehension.

Edm. [*Aside*] If I find him comforting the King, it will stuff his suspicion more fully. [*Aloud*] I will per- severe in my course of loyalty, though the conflict be 20 sore between that and my blood.

Corn. I will lay trust upon thee, and thou shalt find a dearer father in my love.

Exeunt.

III. vi. Sheltered in a farmhouse on Gloucester's lands, Lear, now mad, convenes a court composed of Edgar, the Fool, and Kent to try his daughters. Gloucester returns to warn them that the King's life is in danger and orders Kent to place the King in a litter and flee toward Dover.

|||||||||||||||||||||||||||||||||||||

6. **Frateretto:** another fiend

15-6. **To have a thousand with red burning spits/ Come hizzing in upon 'em:** Lear imagines fiends torturing his daughters.

16. **hizzing:** hissing, suggesting the sound of the hot spits

20. **them:** Goneril and Regan

Scene VI. [An outbuilding near Gloucester's Castle.]

Enter *Gloucester* and *Kent*.

Glou. Here is better than the open air; take it thank-
fully. I will piece out the comfort with what addition I
can. I will not be long from you.

Kent. All the power of his wits have given way to his
impatience. The gods reward your kindness!   5

Exit [*Gloucester*].

[Enter *Lear, Edgar,* and *Fool.*]

Edg. Frateretto calls me, and tells me Nero is an angler
in the lake of darkness. Pray, innocent, and beware the
foul fiend.

Fool. Prithee, nuncle, tell me whether a madman be a
gentleman or a yeoman.   10

Lear. A king, a king!

Fool. No, he's a yeoman that has a gentleman to his
son; for he's a mad yeoman that sees his son a gentleman
before him.

Lear. To have a thousand with red burning spits   15
Come hizzing in upon 'em—

Edg. The foul fiend bites my back.

Fool. He's mad that trusts in the tameness of a wolf,
a horse's health, a boy's love, or a whore's oath.

Lear. It shall be done; I will arraign them straight.   20
[*To Edgar*] Come, sit thou here, most learned justicer.
[*To the Fool*] Thou, sapient sir, sit here. Now, you she-
    foxes!

24. **Look where he stands and glares:** Edgar refers to a fiend supposedly looking on.

26. **Come o'er the bourn, Bessy, to me:** the refrain of a song, addressed playfully here to Lear's daughter as though she were present; **bourn:** brook

31. **Hoppedance:** Hoberdidance, one of Harsnett's devils, probably spelled thus in remembrance of a passage in Harsnett concerning the interpretation of noise from the stomach as the devil in the form of a toad croaking

34. **amazed:** dumfounded

44. **for one blast:** for the time it takes you to blow one blast; **minikin:** delicate, dainty, diminutive, and probably here, shrill

46. **Purr! the cat is grey:** one of Harsnett's demons is so called. Edgar pretends to see a devil in the form of a cat.

52. **joint-stool:** a stool made by a joiner, better than a carpenter's workmanship. "Cry you mercy, I took you for a joint-stool" was a proverbial phrase used as a facetious apology for overlooking a person's presence. In this case, the person is really a joint-stool.

55. **store:** material

Edg. Look, where he stands and glares! Wantest thou
eyes at trial, madam?   25
        Come o'er the bourn, Bessy, to me.

Fool.   Her boat hath a leak,
        And she must not speak
      Why she dares not come over to thee.

Edg. The foul fiend haunts poor Tom in the voice of a   30
nightingale. Hoppedance cries in Tom's belly for two
white herring. Croak not, black angel; I have no food for
thee.

Kent. How do you, sir? Stand you not so amazed.
Will you lie down and rest upon the cushions?   35

Lear. I'll see their trial first. Bring in their evidence.
[*To Edgar*] Thou, robed man of justice, take thy place.
[*To the Fool*] And thou, his yokefellow of equity,
Bench by his side. [*To Kent*] You are o' the commission,
Sit you too.   40

Edg. Let us deal justly.
      Sleepest or wakest thou, jolly shepherd?
        Thy sheep be in the corn;
     And for one blast of thy minikin mouth
        Thy sheep shall take no harm.   45
Purr! the cat is grey.

Lear. Arraign her first. 'Tis Goneril. I here take my
oath before this honorable assembly, she kicked the poor
King her father.

Fool. Come hither, mistress. Is your name Goneril?   50

Lear. She cannot deny it.

Fool. Cry you mercy, I took you for a joint-stool.

Lear. And here's another, whose warped looks pro-
    claim
What store her heart is made on. Stop her there!   55

"Tom O'Bedlam." Woodcut illustration for an old ballad.
(See III. vi. 76.)

70. **brach:** hound bitch; see I. iv. 110. **lym:** lyam or lymmer, a kind of bloodhound

71. **tyke:** a mongrel; **trundle-tail:** a dog with a long curled tail

75. **Sessa:** see III. iv. 105. **wakes:** church festivals

76. **thy horn is dry:** the typical Bedlam beggar wore a horn which he would attempt to fill by repeating this formula at inns and private dwellings. Edgar is saying at the same time that his inspiration in playing Poor Tom is wearing thin.

77. **anatomize:** dissect

79. **entertain:** take on, hire

81. **Persian:** an ironic comment on Edgar's raggedness, since Persian dress was considered very splendid and colorful.

Arms, arms! sword! fire! Corruption in the place!
False justicer, why hast thou let her scape?

 Edg. Bless thy five wits!

 Kent. O pity! Sir, where is the patience now
That you so oft have boasted to retain?   60

 Edg. [*Aside*] My tears begin to take his part so much
They mar my counterfeiting.

 Lear. The little dogs and all,
Tray, Blanch, and Sweetheart, see, they bark at me.

 Edg. Tom will throw his head at them. Avaunt, you   65
curs!

> Be thy mouth or black or white,
> Tooth that poisons if it bite;
> Mastiff, greyhound, mongrel grim,
> Hound or spaniel, brach or lym,   70
> Bobtail tyke or trundle-tail—
> Tom will make him weep and wail;
> For, with throwing thus my head,
> Dogs leap the hatch, and all are fled.

Do de, de, de. Sessa! Come, march to wakes and fairs   75
and market towns. Poor Tom, thy horn is dry.

 Lear. Then let them anatomize Regan. See what breeds
about her heart. Is there any cause in nature that makes
these hard hearts? [*To Edgar*] You, sir, I entertain for one
of my hundred; only I do not like the fashion of your gar-   80
ments. You'll say they are Persian; but let them be
changed.

 Kent. Now, good my lord, lie here and rest awhile.

 Lear. Make no noise, make no noise; draw the curtains.
So, so. We'll go to supper i' the morning.   85

 Fool. And I'll go to bed at noon.

97. **Stand in assured loss:** are threatened with certain loss

103. **Stand in hard cure:** will be difficult to cure

109. **Who alone suffers suffers most i' the mind:** one who has no example of the suffering of others, suffers greater mental anguish.

111. **sufferance:** suffering

112. **bearing:** endurance

Enter *Gloucester*.

Glou. Come hither, friend. Where is the King my master?

Kent. Here, sir; but trouble him not; his wits are gone.

Glou. Good friend, I prithee take him in thy arms.　90
I have o'erheard a plot of death upon him.
There is a litter ready; lay him in it
And drive toward Dover, friend, where thou shalt meet
Both welcome and protection. Take up thy master.
If thou shouldst dally half an hour, his life,　95
With thine, and all that offer to defend him,
Stand in assured loss. Take up, take up!
And follow me, that will to some provision
Give thee quick conduct.

Kent.　　　　　　　Oppressed nature sleeps.　100
This rest might yet have balmed thy broken sinews
Which, if convenience will not allow,
Stand in hard cure. [*To the Fool*] Come, help to bear thy master.
Thou must not stay behind.　105

Glou.　　　　　　　Come, come, away!
　　　　　　　　Exeunt [*all but Edgar*].

Edg. When we our betters see bearing our woes,
We scarcely think our miseries our foes.
Who alone suffers suffers most i' the mind,
Leaving free things and happy shows behind;　110
But then the mind much sufferance doth o'erskip
When grief hath mates, and bearing fellowship.
How light and portable my pain seems now,
When that which makes me bend makes the King bow,
He childed as I fathered! Tom, away!　115

116. **Mark the high noises:** note the discords in high places; **bewray:** expose; see II. i. 116.

118. **repeals and reconciles thee:** repeals the verdict against you and reconciles you with your father

IIIIIIIIIIIIIIIIIIIIIIIIIIIIIIIIIIIIIIIIIIIIIIIIIIIIIII

III. vii. Cornwall and Regan confront Gloucester. After a skirmish in which a servant wounds him, Cornwall plucks out Gloucester's eyes and thrusts him out to "smell his way to Dover."

IIIIIIIIIIIIIIIIIIIIIIIIIIIIIIIIIIIIIIIIII

9-10. **to a most festinate preparation:** to prepare speedily for war; **festinate:** hasty, from the Latin *festinare*

10. **bound to the like:** intend the same preparation

11. **intelligent:** well informed

16. **questrists:** pursuers

Mark the high noises, and thyself bewray
When false opinion, whose wrong thoughts defile thee,
In thy just proof repeals and reconciles thee.
What will hap more tonight, safe scape the King!
Lurk, lurk.   [*Exit.*]   120

————————————————————————————————

Scene VII. [Inside Gloucester's Castle.]

Enter *Cornwall, Regan, Goneril,* [*Edmund* the]
Bastard, and *Servants.*

Corn. [*To Goneril*] Post speedily to my lord your husband, show him this letter. The army of France is landed.
—Seek out the traitor Gloucester.
               [*Exeunt some of the Servants.*]
Reg. Hang him instantly.
Gon. Pluck out his eyes.   5
Corn. Leave him to my displeasure. Edmund, keep
you our sister company. The revenges we are bound to
take upon your traitorous father are not fit for your be-
holding. Advise the Duke where you are going, to a most
festinate preparation. We are bound to the like. Our posts   10
shall be swift and intelligent betwixt us. Farewell, dear
sister; farewell, my Lord of Gloucester.

Enter [*Oswald* the] *Steward.*

How now? Where's the King?
Osw. My Lord of Gloucester hath conveyed him hence.
Some five or six and thirty of his knights,   15
Hot questrists after him, met him at gate;

26-7. **our power/ Shall do a court'sy to our wrath:** our legal power shall bow to our anger.

32. **corky:** withered and sapless

Who, with some other of the lord's dependants,
Are gone with him toward Dover, where they boast
To have well-armed friends.
    Corn.   Get horses for your mistress.   20
    Gon. Farewell, sweet lord, and sister.
    Corn. Edmund, farewell.
            Exeunt Goneril, [Edmund, and Oswald].
                Go seek the traitor Gloucester,
Pinion him like a thief, bring him before us.
                  [Exeunt other Servants.]
Though well we may not pass upon his life   25
Without the form of justice, yet our power
Shall do a court'sy to our wrath, which men
May blame, but not control.

    Enter *Gloucester*, brought in by two or three.

                Who's there? the traitor?   30
    Reg. Ingrateful fox! 'tis he.
    Corn. Bind fast his corky arms.
    Glou. What mean your Graces? Good my friends, consider
You are my guests. Do me no foul play, friends.   35
    Corn. Bind him, I say.
                  [Servants bind him.]
    Reg.   Hard, hard. O filthy traitor!
    Glou. Unmerciful lady as you are, I am none.
    Corn. To this chair bind him. Villain, thou shalt find—
                [Regan pulls his beard.]
    Glou. By the kind gods, 'tis most ignobly done   40
To pluck me by the beard.
    Reg. So white, and such a traitor!

45. **quicken**: come alive

47. **ruffle**: violently outrage

51. **Late footed**: recently landed

54. **guessingly set down**: expressing speculation rather than certainty

64-5. **I am tied to the stake, and I must stand the course**: Gloucester compares his situation with that of a bear about to be baited: tied to a post and unable to repel the attacks of dogs set upon him.

69. **rash**: slash as a boar with his tusks

71-2. **buoyed up/ And quenched the stelled fires**: swelled to the heavens and extinguished the stars

73. **holp**: helped

74. **dern**: dark, dreadful

Glou.   Naughty lady,
These hairs which thou dost ravish from my chin
Will quicken, and accuse thee. I am your host.   45
With robber's hands my hospitable favors
You should not ruffle thus. What will you do?
   Corn. Come, sir, what letters had you late from France?
   Reg. Be simple-answered, for we know the truth.
   Corn. And what confederacy have you with the traitors   50
Late footed in the kingdom?
   Reg. To whose hands you have sent the lunatic King?
Speak.
   Glou.   I have a letter guessingly set down,
Which came from one that's of a neutral heart,   55
And not from one opposed.
   Corn.   Cunning.
   Reg.   And false.
   Corn. Where hast thou sent the King?
   Glou. To Dover.   60
   Reg. Wherefore to Dover? Wast thou not charged at
      peril—
   Corn. Wherefore to Dover? Let him answer that.
   Glou. I am tied to the stake, and I must stand the
      course.   65
   Reg. Wherefore to Dover?
   Glou. Because I would not see thy cruel nails
Pluck out his poor old eyes; nor thy fierce sister
In his anointed flesh rash boarish fangs.
The sea, with such a storm as his bare head   70
In hell-black night endured, would have buoyed up
And quenched the stelled fires.
Yet, poor old heart, he holp the heavens to rain.
If wolves had at thy gate howled that dern time,
Thou shouldst have said, "Good porter, turn the key."   75

76. **All cruels else subscribe:** disregard all your other cruelties.

77. **winged vengeance:** divine vengeance

80. **will think to:** hopes or expects to

102. **sparks of nature:** filial affection

103. **quit:** requite

105. **overture:** disclosure

All cruels else subscribe: but I shall see
The winged vengeance overtake such children.
  Corn. See it shalt thou never. Fellows, hold the chair.
Upon these eyes of thine I'll set my foot.
  Glou. He that will think to live till he be old,   80
Give me some help!—O cruel! O you gods!
  Reg. One side will mock another. The other too!
  Corn. If you see vengeance—
  1. Serv.   Hold your hand, my lord!
I have served you ever since I was a child,   85
But better service have I never done you
Than now to bid you hold.
  Reg.   How now, you dog?
  1. Serv. If you did wear a beard upon your chin,
I'd shake it on this quarrel.   90
  Reg.   What do you mean?
  Corn. My villain!   *[They] draw and fight.*
  1. Serv. Nay, then, come on, and take the chance of
    anger.
  Reg. Give me thy sword. A peasant stand up thus?   95
          She takes a sword and runs at him behind.
  1. Serv. O, I am slain! My lord, you have one eye left
To see some mischief on him. O!   *He dies.*
  Corn. Lest it see more, prevent it. Out, vile jelly!
Where is thy lustre now?
  Glou. All dark and comfortless! Where's my son Ed-   100
    mund?
Edmund, enkindle all the sparks of nature
To quit this horrid act.
  Reg.   Out, treacherous villain!
Thou callest on him that hates thee. It was he
That made the overture of thy treasons to us,   105
Who is too good to pity thee.

111. **How look you:** how are things with you.

119. **meet the old course of death:** die naturally

121. **bedlam:** referring to Edgar

122-23. **His roguish madness/ Allows itself to anything:** as a mad wanderer he is available for any errand.

124. **flax and whites of eggs:** a contemporary remedy for an injury

Glou. O my follies! Then Edgar was abused.
Kind gods, forgive me that, and prosper him!
  Reg. Go thrust him out at gates, and let him smell
His way to Dover.   110

                    Exit [a Servant] with Gloucester.
                    How is't, my lord? How look you?
  Corn. I have received a hurt. Follow me, lady.
Turn out that eyeless villain. Throw this slave
Upon the dunghill. Regan, I bleed apace.
Untimely comes this hurt. Give me your arm.   115

                    Exit [Cornwall, led by Regan].
  2. Serv. I'll never care what wickedness I do,
If this man come to good.
  3. Serv.   If she live long,
And in the end meet the old course of death,
Women will all turn monsters.   120
  2. Serv. Let's follow the old Earl, and get the bedlam
To lead him where he would. His roguish madness
Allows itself to anything.
  3. Serv. Go thou. I'll fetch some flax and whites of eggs
To apply to his bleeding face. Now heaven help him!   125

                                      Exeunt.

KING LEAR

ACT IV

IV. i. Blind Gloucester, led by an old man on the heath, encounters Edgar, who undertakes to lead him to Dover.

᠁᠁᠁᠁᠁᠁᠁᠁᠁᠁᠁

1-2. **Yet better thus, and known to be contemned,/ Than still contemned and flattered:** better to be thus conscious of scorn than to be apparently secure and the target of hostility concealed by flattery.

4. **esperance:** hope

6. **The worst returns to laughter:** when at the worst, any change in one's condition must be in the direction of happiness.

12-3. **But that thy strange mutations make us hate thee,/ Life would not yield to age:** if your capriciousness did not make us hate you, men would not age and die.

ACT IV

Scene I. [The heath.]

Enter *Edgar*.

Edg. Yet better thus, and known to be contemned,
Than still contemned and flattered. To be worst,
The lowest and most dejected thing of fortune,
Stands still in esperance, lives not in fear.
The lamentable change is from the best;   5
The worst returns to laughter. Welcome then,
Thou unsubstantial air that I embrace!
The wretch that thou hast blown unto the worst
Owes nothing to thy blasts.

Enter *Gloucester*, led by an *Old Man*.

                        But who comes here?   10
My father, poorly led? World, world, O world!
But that thy strange mutations make us hate thee,
Life would not yield to age.
    Old Man.   O my good lord,
I have been your tenant, and your father's tenant,   15
These fourscore years.

22. **stumbled**: that is, into error; failed to recognize truth

23-4. **Our means secure us, and our mere defects/ Prove our commodities**: our material advantages provide only false security and our misfortunes turn out to be benefits. "Secure" is used in the opposite sense of making secure, that is, making reckless and thus exposing to danger.

25. **food**: object; **abused**: deceived; see I. iii. 21.

33-4. **The worst is not/ So long as we can say "This is the worst"**: We have not reached the worst if we have hope enough to consider that nothing worse can come.

38. **He has some reason, else he could not beg**: he at least has enough sense to be aware of his physical needs.

Glou. Away, get thee away! Good friend, be gone.
Thy comforts can do me no good at all;
Thee they may hurt.

    Old Man.   You cannot see your way.   20

    Glou. I have no way, and therefore want no eyes;
I stumbled when I saw. Full oft 'tis seen
Our means secure us, and our mere defects
Prove our commodities. O dear son Edgar,
The food of thy abused father's wrath;   25
Might I but live to see thee in my touch,
I'd say I had eyes again!

    Old Man.   How now? Who's there?

    Edg. [*Aside*] O gods! Who is't can say "I am at the
    worst"?   30
I am worse than e'er I was.

    Old Man.   'Tis poor mad Tom.

    Edg. [*Aside*] And worse I may be yet. The worst is not
So long as we can say "This is the worst."

    Old Man. Fellow, where goest?   35

    Glou.   Is it a beggarman?

    Old Man. Madman and beggar too.

    Glou. He has some reason, else he could not beg.
I' the last night's storm I such a fellow saw,
Which made me think a man a worm. My son   40
Came then into my mind, and yet my mind
Was then scarce friends with him. I have heard more
    since.
As flies to wanton boys are we to the gods.
They kill us for their sport.   45

    Edg.   [*Aside*] How should this be?
Bad is the trade that must play fool to sorrow,
Angering itself and others.—Bless thee, master!

    Glou. Is that the naked fellow?

61. **'parel**: apparel

64-5. **I cannot daub it further**: I cannot maintain this role; **daub**: plaster, by extension, to cover with something in order to conceal its real nature

73. **Obidicut**: Hoberdicut in Harsnett

75. **mopping and mowing**: making wry mouths, grimacing. Edgar suggests that Flibbertigibbet may be responsible for the facial distortions of affected women trying to imitate women of fashion. The possession by devils of three chambermaids is commented on in Harsnett.

82. **superfluous**: possessing more than enough; **lust-dieted**: practically synonymous with superfluous

Old Man.   Ay, my lord.   50

  Glou. Get thee away. If for my sake
Thou wilt o'ertake us hence a mile or twain
I' the way toward Dover, do it for ancient love;
And bring some covering for this naked soul,
Which I'll entreat to lead me.   55

  Old Man.   Alack, sir, he is mad!

  Glou. 'Tis the time's plague when madmen lead the
    blind.
Do as I bid thee, or rather do thy pleasure.
Above the rest, be gone.   60

  Old Man. I'll bring him the best 'parel that I have,
Come on't what will.   *Exit.*

  Glou. Sirrah naked fellow—

  Edg. Poor Tom's acold. [*Aside*] I cannot daub it
    further.   65

  Glou. Come hither, fellow.

  Edg. [*Aside*] And yet I must.—Bless thy sweet eyes,
    they bleed.

  Glou. Knowest thou the way to Dover?

  Edg. Both stile and gate, horseway and footpath. Poor 70
Tom hath been scared out of his good wits. Bless thee,
good man's son, from the foul fiend! Five fiends have
been in poor Tom at once: of lust, as Obidicut; Hobbi-
didence, prince of dumbness; Mahu, of stealing; Modo,
of murder; Flibbertigibbet, of mopping and mowing, who 75
since possesses chambermaids and waiting women. So,
bless thee, master!

  Glou. Here, take this purse, thou whom the heavens'
    plagues
Have humbled to all strokes. That I am wretched 80
Makes thee the happier. Heavens, deal so still!
Let the superfluous and lust-dieted man,

83. **slaves your ordinance**: behaves as though the good fortune you have ordained were his due

92. **something rich about me**: a valuable in my possession

||||||||||||||||||||||||||||||||||||||||||||||||||||||||||||

IV. ii. Edmund accompanies Goneril to the approach to the Duke of Albany's palace. A servant reports that Albany has changed greatly and reacted strangely to Edmund's report of Gloucester's treachery. Goneril thereupon reveals that she loves Edmund and sends him back to Regan. Albany berates Goneril for her cruelty and receives the news of the blinding of Gloucester and the death of Cornwall from the wound received in the fray with his servant. Goneril reveals a fear that Regan will take her lover, Edmund.

||||||||||||||||||||||||||||||||||||||

That slaves your ordinance, that will not see
Because he does not feel, feel your power quickly;
So distribution should undo excess,   85
And each man have enough. Dost thou know Dover?
  Edg. Ay, master.
  Glou. There is a cliff, whose high and bending head
Looks fearfully in the confined deep.
Bring me but to the very brim of it,   90
And I'll repair the misery thou dost bear
With something rich about me. From that place
I shall no leading need.
  Edg.   Give me thy arm.
Poor Tom shall lead thee.   95
                                          Exeunt.

Scene II. [Outside the Duke of Albany's Palace.]

Enter *Goneril* and [*Edmund* the] *Bastard.*

  Gon. Welcome, my lord. I marvel our mild husband
Not met us on the way.

Enter [*Oswald* the] *Steward.*

                    Now where's your master?
  Osw. Madam, within, but never man so changed.
I told him of the army that was landed: 5
He smiled at it. I told him you were coming:
His answer was, "The worse." Of Gloucester's treachery
And of the loyal service of his son

9. **sot**: blockhead, rather than drunkard as in modern usage

14. **cowish**: cowardly

15-6. **He'll not feel wrongs/ Which tie him to an answer**: he overlooks injuries so that he need not revenge them.

19. **arms**: the symbols of male and female: the sword and distaff

27. **Conceive**: understand (me)

32. **My fool**: that is, her husband

34. **I have been worth the whistle**: Goneril implies that at one time her husband thought more highly of her and would have met her on the way.

38. **it**: its

When I informed him, then he called me sot
And told me I had turned the wrong side out.   10
What most he should dislike seems pleasant to him;
What like, offensive.
   Gon. [*To Edmund*] Then shall you go no further.
It is the cowish terror of his spirit,
That dares not undertake. He'll not feel wrongs   15
Which tie him to an answer. Our wishes on the way
May prove effects. Back, Edmund, to my brother.
Hasten his musters and conduct his powers.
I must change arms at home and give the distaff
Into my husband's hands. This trusty servant   20
Shall pass between us. Ere long you are like to hear
(If you dare venture in your own behalf)
A mistress's command. Wear this;   [*Gives a favor.*]
                          Spare speech;
Decline your head: this kiss, if it durst speak,   25
Would stretch thy spirits up into the air.
Conceive, and fare thee well.
   Edm. Yours in the ranks of death!   *Exit.*
   Gon.   My most dear Gloucester!
O, the difference of man and man!   30
To thee a woman's services are due;
My fool usurps my body.
   Osw.   Madam, here comes my lord.   *Exit.*

Enter *Albany.*

   Gon. I have been worth the whistle.
   Alb.   O Goneril,   35
You are not worth the dust which the rude wind
Blows in your face! I fear your disposition.
That nature which contemns it origin

40. **sliver and disbranch:** sever

41. **material sap:** vital nourishment, that is, from the parent to whom she owes her existence

48. **head-lugged:** dragged by the head, i.e., sulky

59-60. **discerning/ Thine honor from thy suffering:** discriminating between what a man must bear and what he should resent for his honor's sake

61-2. **Fools do those villains pity who are punished/ Ere they have done their mischief:** only a fool pities a villain because he is punished before he is able to do wrong.

64. **helm:** helmet

65. **moral:** hesitating on fine points of morality

68-9. **Proper deformity shows not in the fiend/ So horrid as in woman:** deformity being appropriate to a fiend, it is not so repulsive as in a woman.

70. **vain:** useless

71. **changed and self-covered thing:** Goneril is allowing her evil temper to distort her face, but it is her own nature which has transformed her; otherwise one might think a fiend had assumed her body.

Cannot be bordered certain in itself.
She that herself will sliver and disbranch 40
From her material sap, perforce must wither
And come to deadly use.
   Gon. No more! The text is foolish.
   Alb. Wisdom and goodness to the vile seem vile;
Filths savor but themselves. What have you done? 45
Tigers, not daughters, what have you performed?
A father, and a gracious aged man,
Whose reverence even the head-lugged bear would lick,
Most barbarous, most degenerate, have you madded.
Could my good brother suffer you to do it? 50
A man, a prince, by him so benefited!
If that the heavens do not their visible spirits
Send quickly down to tame these vile offenses,
It will come,
Humanity must perforce prey on itself, 55
Like monsters of the deep.
   Gon.   Milk-livered man!
That bearest a cheek for blows, a head for wrongs;
Who hast not in thy brows an eye discerning
Thine honor from thy suffering; that not knowest 60
Fools do those villains pity who are punished
Ere they have done their mischief. Where's thy drum?
France spreads his banners in our noiseless land,
With plumed helm thy state begins to threat,
Whiles thou, a moral fool, sittest still, and cries 65
"Alack, why does he so?"
   Alb.   See thyself, devil!
Proper deformity shows not in the fiend
So horrid as in woman.
   Gon.   O vain fool! 70
   Alb. Thou changed and self-covered thing, for shame!

72. **Were't my fitness**: if it were fitting for me (as a man)

73. **my blood**: my impulse to violence

77. **mew**: editors disagree as to the meaning of "mew" here, but to the present editors it appears likely to be a mere exclamation of contempt. Clearly, Goneril is expressing contempt for the quality of Albany's manhood.

90. **nether**: committed below on earth, worldly

98-9. **May all the building in my fancy pluck/ Upon my hateful life**: may pull down my castle in the air and destroy me

Bemonster not thy feature! Were't my fitness
To let these hands obey my blood,
They are apt enough to dislocate and tear
Thy flesh and bones. Howe'er thou art a fiend,   75
A woman's shape doth shield thee.
   Gon. Marry, your manhood—mew!

            Enter a *Gentleman.*

   Alb. What news?
   Gent. O, my good lord, the Duke of Cornwall's dead,
Slain by his servant, going to put out   80
The other eye of Gloucester.
   Alb.   Gloucester's eyes?
   Gent. A servant that he bred, thrilled with remorse,
Opposed against the act, bending his sword
To his great master; who, thereat enraged,   85
Flew on him, and amongst them felled him dead;
But not without that harmful stroke which since
Hath plucked him after.
   Alb.   This shows you are above,
You justicers, that these our nether crimes   90
So speedily can venge! But O poor Gloucester!
Lost he his other eye?
   Gent.   Both, both, my lord.
This letter, madam, craves a speedy answer.
'Tis from your sister.   95
   Gon.   [*Aside*] One way I like this well;
But being widow, and my Gloucester with her,
May all the building in my fancy pluck
Upon my hateful life. Another way
The news is not so tart.—I'll read, and answer.   100
                       Exit.

104. **back again:** on his way back

‖‖

IV. [iii.] Kent reaches the French camp near Dover and discovers that an emergency has recalled the King of France but that Cordelia remains with the troops. Lear, conscience-stricken at his wrongs to her, will not yet consent to see Cordelia.

‖‖‖‖‖‖‖‖‖‖‖‖‖‖‖‖‖‖‖‖‖‖‖‖‖‖‖‖‖‖‖‖‖‖‖‖

4. **imports:** portends

Alb. Where was his son when they did take his eyes?
Gent. Come with my lady hither.
Alb.   He is not here.
Gent. No, my good lord; I met him back again.
Alb. Knows he the wickedness?   105
Gent. Ay, my good lord: 'twas he informed against
   him,
And quit the house on purpose, that their punishment
Might have the freer course.
Alb.   Gloucester, I live   110
To thank thee for the love thou show'dst the King,
And to revenge thine eyes. Come hither, friend.
Tell me what more thou knowest.
                                        Exeunt.

[Scene III. The French camp near Dover.]

Enter *Kent* and a *Gentleman*.

Kent. Why the King of France is so suddenly gone
back; know you no reason?
Gent. Something he left imperfect in the state, which
since his coming forth is thought of, which imports to the
kingdom so much fear and danger that his personal return   5
was most required and necessary.
Kent. Who hath he left behind him general?
Gent. The Marshal of France, Monsieur La Far.
Kent. Did your letters pierce the Queen to any demon-
stration of grief?   10

19. **express her goodliest:** best become her

26. **If all could so become it:** if it were as becoming to all

35. **clamor moistened:** her excited words were moistened by tears

39. **make:** mate

Gent. Ay, sir. She took them, read them in my pres-
ence,
And now and then an ample tear trilled down
Her delicate cheek. It seemed she was a queen
Over her passion, who, most rebel-like,   15
Sought to be king o'er her.
    Kent.   O, then it moved her?
    Gent. Not to a rage. Patience and sorrow strove
Who should express her goodliest. You have seen
Sunshine and rain at once: her smiles and tears   20
Were like. A better way: those happy smilets
That played on her ripe lip seemed not to know
What guests were in her eyes, which parted thence
As pearls from diamonds dropped. In brief,
Sorrow would be a rarity most beloved,   25
If all could so become it.
    Kent.   Made she no verbal question?
    Gent. Faith, once or twice she heaved the name of
father
Pantingly forth, as if it pressed her heart;   30
Cried "Sisters, sisters! Shame of ladies! Sisters!
Kent! father! sisters! What, i' the storm? i' the night?
Let pity not be believed!" There she shook
The holy water from her heavenly eyes,
And clamor moistened. Then away she started   35
To deal with grief alone.
    Kent.   It is the stars,
The stars above us, govern our conditions;
Else one self mate and make could not beget
Such different issues. You spoke not with her since?   40
    Gent. No.
    Kent. Was this before the King returned?
    Gent.   No, since.

45. **in his better tune:** in moments of greater rationality

49. **sovereign:** overpowering; **elbows him:** attends him closely

52. **dear:** important

63. **grieve:** regret

64. **Lending me this acquaintance:** having associated with me

      ||||||||||||||||||||||||||||||||||||||||||||||||||||||||

IV. [**iv.**] Cordelia learns of Lear's condition and sends soldiers to seek him out, instructing her doctor to attempt his cure. She prepares for the approach of the enemy forces.

      ||||||||||||||||||||||||||||||||||||

3. **fumiter:** fumitory, any plant of the genus *Fumaria,* especially *F. officinalis*

Kent. Well, sir, the poor distressed Lear's i' the town;
Who sometime, in his better tune, remembers   45
What we are come about, and by no means
Will yield to see his daughter.
    Gent.   Why, good sir?
    Kent. A sovereign shame so elbows him; his own un-
      kindness,   50
That stripped her from his benediction, turned her
To foreign casualties, gave her dear rights
To his dog-hearted daughters—these things sting
His mind so venomously that burning shame
Detains him from Cordelia.   55
    Gent.   Alack, poor gentleman!
    Kent. Of Albany's and Cornwall's powers you heard
      not?
    Gent. 'Tis so; they are afoot.
    Kent. Well, sir, I'll bring you to our master Lear   60
And leave you to attend him. Some dear cause
Will in concealment wrap me up awhile.
When I am known aright, you shall not grieve
Lending me this acquaintance. I pray you go
Along with me.   *Exeunt.*   65

Scene [IV. Same.]

Enter, with *Drum* and *Colors, Cordelia, Doctor,* and
Soldiers.

Cor. Alack, 'tis he! Why, he was met even now
As mad as the vexed sea, singing aloud,
Crowned with rank fumiter and furrow-weeds,

4. **hardocks:** variously identified as hoardocks, bur-docks, etc., but evidently some type of coarse weed

5. **Darnel:** a term for any harmful weed

6. **century:** a body of one hundred soldiers

8-9. **What can man's wisdom:** what can science do.

15. **simples:** herbal remedies

18. **unpublished virtues of the earth:** little-known medicinal plants

19. **aidant:** helpful; **remediate:** curative

21. **rage:** delirious frenzy

29. **importuned:** importunate

30. **blown:** inflated

With hardocks, hemlock, nettles, cuckoo-flowers,
Darnel, and all the idle weeds that grow   5
In our sustaining corn. A century send forth.
Search every acre in the high-grown field
And bring him to our eye. [*Exit an Officer.*] What can
     man's wisdom
In the restoring his bereaved sense?   10
He that helps him take all my outward worth.
    Doct. There is means, madam.
Our foster nurse of nature is repose,
The which he lacks. That to provoke in him
Are many simples operative, whose power   15
Will close the eye of anguish.
    Cor.   All blest secrets,
All you unpublished virtues of the earth,
Spring with my tears! be aidant and remediate
In the good man's distress! Seek, seek for him!   20
Lest his ungoverned rage dissolve the life
That wants the means to lead it.

Enter Messenger.

    Mess.   News, madam.
The British powers are marching hitherward.
    Cor. 'Tis known before. Our preparation stands   25
In expectation of them. O dear father,
It is thy business that I go about.
Therefore great France
My mourning and importuned tears hath pitied.
No blown ambition doth our arms incite,   30
But love, dear love, and our aged father's right.
Soon may I hear and see him!
Exeunt.

IV. [v.] Oswald arrives at Gloucester's castle with a letter from Goneril for Edmund, but Regan, jealous of her sister, tries to prevent Oswald from delivering it and instructs him to report her own love for Edmund—and to kill old Gloucester if he should encounter him.

||||||||||||||||||||||||||||||||||||

4. **with much ado:** presumably, "with much indecision and delay," since Albany is not convinced of the right of his own side

15. **nighted:** darkened (by blindness)

24. **Belike:** probably

Scene [V. Inside Gloucester's Castle.]

Enter *Regan* and [*Oswald* the] *Steward*.

Reg. But are my brother's powers set forth?
Osw.   Ay, madam.
Reg. Himself in person there?
Osw.   Madam, with much ado:
Your sister is the better soldier.   5
   Reg. Lord Edmund spake not with your lord at home?
Osw. No, madam.
   Reg. What might import my sister's letter to him?
Osw. I know not, lady.
   Reg. Faith, he is posted hence on serious matter.   10
It was great ignorance, Gloucester's eyes being out,
To let him live. Where he arrives he moves
All hearts against us. Edmund, I think, is gone,
In pity of his misery, to dispatch
His nighted life; moreover, to descry   15
The strength o' the enemy.
   Osw. I must needs after him, madam, with my letter.
   Reg. Our troops set forth tomorrow. Stay with us.
The ways are dangerous.
   Osw.   I may not, madam.   20
My lady charged my duty in this business.
   Reg. Why should she write to Edmund? Might not
      you
Transport her purposes by word? Belike,
Some things—I know not what—I'll love thee much—   25
Let me unseal the letter.
   Osw.   Madam, I had rather—

30. **eliads**: oeillades, amorous glances
31. **of her bosom**: in her confidence
34. **take this note**: note what I say
37. **You may gather more**: you may guess more
than I dare say.

IIIIIIIIIIIIIIIIIIIIIIIIIIIIIIIIIIIIIIIIIIIIIIIIIIIIIIII

IV. [vi.] Edgar pretends to lead blind Gloucester
to a precipice near Dover from which Gloucester tries
to jump to his death. Afterward Edgar, pretending
to be another person, convinces Gloucester that he
had jumped from a great height but was saved by a
miracle. Gloucester becomes reconciled to his fate.
At this point Lear appears and rails bitterly upon the
hypocrisy of humankind. One of Cordelia's gentlemen tries to take Lear in charge but he runs from
the stage. Oswald appears and attempts to kill
Gloucester but is slain by Edgar, who finds upon him
Goneril's letter to Edmund urging him to kill Albany
and take her for his own.

IIIIIIIIIIIIIIIIIIIIIIIIIIIIIIIIIIIIIII

Reg. I know your lady does not love her husband;
I am sure of that; and at her late being here
She gave strange eliads and most speaking looks   30
To noble Edmund. I know you are of her bosom.
    Osw. I, madam?
    Reg. I speak in understanding. Y'are! I know't.
Therefore I do advise you take this note.
My lord is dead; Edmund and I have talked,   35
And more convenient is he for my hand
Than for your lady's. You may gather more.
If you do find him, pray you give him this;
And when your mistress hears thus much from you,
I pray desire her call her wisdom to her.   40
So fare you well.
If you do chance to hear of that blind traitor,
Preferment falls on him that cuts him off.
    Osw. Would I could meet him, madam! I should show
What party I do follow.   45
    Reg.   Fare thee well.   *Exeunt.*

Scene [VI. Open country near Dover.]

Enter *Gloucester,* and *Edgar* [clothed as a countryman].

    Glou. When shall I come to the top of that same hill?
    Edg. You do climb up it now. Look how we labor.
    Glou. Methinks the ground is even.
    Edg.   Horrible steep.
Hark, do you hear the sea?   5

A "Country Clown." Edgar may have looked thus in his second
disguise (IV. vi).
From the Trevelyon MS. in the Folger Shakespeare Library

18. **choughs**: birds of the crow family, often applied to jackdaws

19. **gross**: large

20. **sampire**: samphire, a succulent herb which grew on rocky seacliffs. The name is a corruption of "(herbe de) Saint Pierre." It was valued for use in relish.

24. **cock**: cockboat, a small ship's boat

Glou.   No, truly.

Edg. Why, then, your other senses grow imperfect
By your eyes' anguish.

Glou.   So may it be indeed.
Methinks thy voice is altered, and thou speakest   10
In better phrase and matter than thou didst.

Edg. Y'are much deceived. In nothing am I changed
But in my garments.

Glou.   Methinks y'are better spoken.

Edg. Come on, sir; here's the place. Stand still. How   15
    fearful
And dizzy 'tis to cast one's eyes so low!
The crows and choughs that wing the midway air
Show scarce so gross as beetles. Halfway down
Hangs one that gathers sampire—dreadful trade!   20
Methinks he seems no bigger than his head.
The fishermen that walk upon the beach
Appear like mice; and yond tall anchoring bark,
Diminished to her cock; her cock, a buoy
Almost too small for sight. The murmuring surge   25
That on the unnumbered idle pebble chafes
Cannot be heard so high. I'll look no more,
Lest my brain turn, and the deficient sight
Topple down headlong.

Glou.   Set me where you stand.   30

Edg. Give me your hand; you are now within a foot
Of the extreme verge; for all beneath the moon
Would I not leap upright.

Glou.   Let go my hand.
Here, friend, 's another purse; in it a jewel   35
Well worth a poor man's taking. Fairies and gods
Prosper it with thee! Go thou further off;
Bid me farewell, and let me hear thee going.

47. **opposeless**: irresistible

48. **My snuff and loathed part of nature**: the useless remainder of my life

52. **conceit**: imagination

65. **at each**: placed end to end on top of one another

69. **bourn**: boundary (of the sea)

Edg. Now fare ye well, good sir.

Glou.   With all my heart. 40

Edg. [*Aside*] Why I do trifle thus with his despair
Is done to cure it.

Glou.   O you mighty gods!   *He kneels.*

This world I do renounce, and, in your sights,
Shake patiently my great affliction off.   45
If I could bear it longer and not fall
To quarrel with your great opposeless wills,
My snuff and loathed part of nature should
Burn itself out. If Edgar live, O, bless him!
Now, fellow, fare thee well.   50

                    He falls [forward and faints].

Edg.   Gone, sir, farewell.—

And yet I know not how conceit may rob
The treasury of life when life itself
Yields to the theft. Had he been where he thought,
By this had thought been past.—Alive or dead?   55
Ho you, sir! friend! Hear you, sir? Speak!—
Thus might he pass indeed. Yet he revives.
What are you, sir?

Glou.   Away, and let me die.

Edg. Hadst thou been aught but gossamer, feathers, 60
   air,
So many fathom down precipitating,
Thou'dst shivered like an egg; but thou dost breathe;
Hast heavy substance; bleedest not; speakest; art sound.
Ten masts at each make not the altitude   65
Which thou hast perpendicularly fell.
Thy life's a miracle. Speak yet again.

Glou. But have I fallen, or no?

Edg. From the dread summit of this chalky bourn.

70. **shrill-gorged**: shrill-voiced

86. **whelked**: twisted; **enridged**: furrowed

88. **clearest**: purest

88-9. **who make them honors/ Of men's impossibilities**: who win men's honor by performing feats impossible to them

95. **free**: cheerful

97-8. **The safer sense will ne'er accommodate/ His master thus**: sanity would not clothe a man thus.

Look up a-height. The shrill-gorged lark so far   70
Cannot be seen or heard. Do but look up.
    Glou. Alack, I have no eyes!
Is wretchedness deprived that benefit
To end itself by death? 'Twas yet some comfort
When misery could beguile the tyrant's rage   75
And frustrate his proud will.
    Edg.   Give me your arm.
Up—so. How is't? Feel you your legs? You stand.
    Glou. Too well, too well.
    Edg.   This is above all strangeness.   80
Upon the crown o' the cliff what thing was that
Which parted from you?
    Glou.   A poor unfortunate beggar.
    Edg. As I stood here below, methought his eyes
Were two full moons; he had a thousand noses,   85
Horns whelked and waved like the enridged sea:
It was some fiend; therefore, thou happy father,
Think that the clearest gods, who make them honors
Of men's impossibilities, have preserved thee.
    Glou. I do remember now. Henceforth I'll bear   90
Affliction till it do cry out itself
"Enough, enough," and die. That thing you speak of,
I took it for a man. Often 'twould say
"The fiend, the fiend"—he led me to that place.
    Edg. Bear free and patient thoughts.   95

    Enter *Lear,* mad, [garlanded with wild flowers].

                              But who comes here?
The safer sense will ne'er accommodate
His master thus.

99. **coining:** counterfeiting

103. **press money:** paid to a new recruit on enlistment. Lear imagines himself to be an officer recruiting men for military service.

103-4. **crow-keeper:** awkward archer, like an inexperienced boy employed to scare crows away

104. **clothier's yard:** the measure for a standard English arrow

106. **prove it:** test my prowess (signified by the gauntlet)

107. **brown bills:** foot soldiers armed with "brown bills," halberds painted to prevent rust; **well flown, bird:** Lear compares an imaginary arrow's flight to that of a hawk or falcon; **clout:** center of the target

113-14. **I had white hairs in my beard ere the black ones were there:** I was wise as a bearded old man before my beard began to grow.

115-16. **"Ay" and "no" too was no good divinity:** a reference to the biblical injunction to "let your yea, be yea, and your nay, nay, lest ye fall into damnation," Jas. 5:12.

Lear. No, they cannot touch me for coining; 100
I am the King himself.

Edg. O thou side-piercing sight!

Lear. Nature's above art in that respect. There's your press money. That fellow handles his bow like a crow-keeper. Draw me a clothier's yard. Look, look, a mouse! Peace, peace; this piece of toasted cheese will do it. 105 There's my gauntlet; I'll prove it on a giant. Bring up the brown bills. O, well flown, bird! i' the clout, i' the clout! Hewgh! Give the word.

Edg. Sweet marjoram.

Lear. Pass. 110

Glou. I know that voice.

Lear. Ha! Goneril with a white beard? They flattered me like a dog, and told me I had white hairs in my beard ere the black ones were there. To say "ay" and "no" to everything that I said! "Ay" and "no" too was no good 115 divinity. When the rain came to wet me once, and the wind to make me chatter; when the thunder would not peace at my bidding; there I found 'em, there I smelt 'em out. Go to, they are not men o' their words! They told me I was everything. 'Tis a lie—I am not ague-proof. 120

Glou. The trick of that voice I do well remember. Is't not the King?

Lear.   Ay, every inch a king!
When I do stare, see how the subject quakes.
I pardon that man's life. What was thy cause? 125
Adultery?
Thou shalt not die. Die for adultery? No.
The wren goes to it, and the small gilded fly
Does lecher in my sight.
Let copulation thrive; for Gloucester's bastard son 130
Was kinder to his father than my daughters

A crow-keeper.
(See IV. vi. 103-4.)
From the Trevelyon MS. in the Folger Shakespeare Library.

135. **forks:** ornaments for holding up the hair

136. **minces virtue:** affects chastity

138. **fitchew:** polecat, also a cant term for prostitute

150. **piece:** masterpiece

159. **case:** rim, sockets

160. **are you there with me:** is that what you mean.

164. **I see it feelingly:** I perceive it by feeling it, and feel it keenly.

Got 'tween the lawful sheets.
To it, luxury, pell-mell! for I lack soldiers.
Behold yond simpering dame,
Whose face between her forks presages snow, 135
That minces virtue, and does shake the head
To hear of pleasure's name.
The fitchew nor the soiled horse goes to it
With a more riotous appetite.
Down from the waist they are Centaurs, 140
Though women all above.
But to the girdle do the gods inherit,
Beneath is all the fiend's.
There's hell, there's darkness, there is the sulphurous pit;
burning, scalding, stench, consumption. Fie, fie, fie! pah, 145
pah! Give me an ounce of civet; good apothecary,
sweeten my imagination. There's money for thee.

Glou. O, let me kiss that hand!

Lear. Let me wipe it first; it smells of mortality.

Glou. O ruined piece of nature! This great world 150
Shall so wear out to naught. Dost thou know me?

Lear. I remember thine eyes well enough. Dost thou
squint at me? No, do thy worst, blind Cupid! I'll not love.
Read thou this challenge; mark but the penning of it.

Glou. Were all thy letters suns, I could not see. 155

Edg. [*Aside*] I would not take this from report. It is,
And my heart breaks at it.

Lear. Read.

Glou. What, with the case of eyes?

Lear. O, ho, are you there with me? No eyes in your 160
head, nor no money in your purse? Your eyes are in a
heavy case, your purse in a light. Yet you see how this
world goes.

Glou. I see it feelingly.

Elizabethan robed justices.
From the Trevelyon MS. in the Folger Shakespeare Library

168. **handy-dandy**: a children's game involving the choice of either hand for a hidden object

172. **creature**: human being

173. **image**: personification

175. **beadle**: a parish official

179. **cozener**: petty swindler

184. **able**: vouch for

190. **matter and impertinency**: sense and nonsense

Lear. What, art mad? A man may see how this world 165
goes with no eyes. Look with thine ears. See how yond
justice rails upon yond simple thief. Hark in thine ear.
Change places and, handy-dandy, which is the justice,
which is the thief? Thou hast seen a farmer's dog bark
at a beggar? 170

Glou. Ay, sir.

Lear. And the creature run from the cur? There thou
mightst behold the great image of authority: a dog's
obeyed in office.
Thou rascal beadle, hold thy bloody hand! 175
Why dost thou lash that whore? Strip thine own back.
Thou hotly lusts to use her in that kind
For which thou whippest her. The usurer hangs the
    cozener.
Through tattered clothes small vices do appear; 180
Robes and furred gowns hide all. Plate sin with gold,
And the strong lance of justice hurtless breaks;
Arm it in rags, a pygmy's straw does pierce it.
None does offend, none, I say, none; I'll able 'em:
Take that of me, my friend, who have the power 185
To seal th' accuser's lips. Get thee glass eyes
And, like a scurvy politician, seem
To see the things thou dost not. Now, now, now, now!
Pull off my boots. Harder, harder! So.

Edg. O, matter and impertinency mixed! 190
Reason in madness!

Lear. If thou wilt weep my fortunes, take my eyes.
I know thee well enough; thy name is Gloucester.
Thou must be patient. We came crying hither;
Thou knowest, the first time that we smell the air 195
We wawl and cry. I will preach to thee: mark.

Glou. Alack, alack the day!

199. **This' a good block**: it has been conjectured that Lear is handling a hat, real or imaginary, which leads to his mention of felt at l. 201.

200. **delicate**: subtle

207. **natural fool of fortune**: one born to be Fortune's fool

214. **bravely**: Lear is playing on the word "bravely," which connotes both "courageously" and "finely clothed" (an ironic reference to his weed-ornamented rags).

215. **smug**: spruce

219. **Sa, sa, sa, sa**: French çà, çà, "here, here," a cry to urge hounds to the chase

Lear. When we are born, we cry that we are come
To this great stage of fools. This' a good block.
It were a delicate stratagem to shoe   200
A troop of horse with felt. I'll put't in proof,
And when I have stolen upon these sons-in-law,
Then kill, kill, kill, kill, kill, kill!

Enter a *Gentleman* [with *Attendants*].

Gent. O, here he is! Lay hand upon him.—Sir,
Your most dear daughter—   205
Lear. No rescue? What, a prisoner? I am even
The natural fool of fortune. Use me well;
You shall have ransom. Let me have surgeons;
I am cut to the brains.
Gent.   You shall have anything.   210
Lear. No seconds? All myself?
Why, this would make a man a man of salt,
To use his eyes for garden waterpots,
Ay, and laying autumn's dust. I will die bravely,
Like a smug bridegroom. What! I will be jovial.   215
Come, come, I am a king; masters, know you that?
Gent. You are a royal one, and we obey you.
Lear. Then there's life in't. Come, an you get it, you
shall get it by running. Sa, sa, sa, sa!
            Exit running [followed by Attendants].
Gent. A sight most pitiful in the meanest wretch,   220
Past speaking of in a king! Thou hast one daughter
Who redeems nature from the general curse
Which twain have brought her to.
Edg. Hail, gentle sir.
Gent.   Sir, speed you. What's your will?   225

227. **vulgar:** a matter of common knowledge

231-32. **The main descry/ Stands on the hourly thought:** the main force is looked for at any hour.

244. **pregnant to:** susceptible to

245. **biding:** abode

248. **To boot, and boot:** as compensation into the bargain. "To boot" means "in addition," "into the bargain," and "boot" means "premium," "compensation."

252. **Briefly thyself remember:** survey your life and prepare yourself for death.

Edg. Do you hear aught, sir, of a battle toward?

Gent. Most sure and vulgar. Every one hears that
Which can distinguish sound.

Edg.   But, by your favor,
How near's the other army?   230

Gent. Near and on speedy foot. The main descry
Stands on the hourly thought.

Edg.   I thank you, sir. That's all.

Gent. Though that the Queen on special cause is here,
Her army is moved on.   235

Edg.   I thank you, sir.

                         Exit [Gentleman].

Glou. You ever-gentle gods, take my breath from me;
Let not my worser spirit tempt me again
To die before you please!

Edg.   Well pray you, father.   240

Glou. Now, good sir, what are you?

Edg. A most poor man, made tame to fortune's blows,
Who, by the art of known and feeling sorrows,
Am pregnant to good pity. Give me your hand;
I'll lead you to some biding.   245

Glou.   Hearty thanks.
The bounty and the benison of heaven
To boot, and boot!

           Enter [*Oswald* the] *Steward.*

Osw.   A proclaimed prize! Most happy!
That eyeless head of thine was first framed flesh   250
To raise my fortunes. Thou old unhappy traitor,
Briefly thyself remember: the sword is out
That must destroy thee.

260-70. Edgar adopts a rustic dialect in keeping with his new disguise.

260. **Chill**: I will; **'casion**: occasion

263. **chud**: I would.

265. **che vor' ye**: I warn you.

266. **Ise**: I shall; **costard**: a kind of apple of large size, applied humorously to the head; **ballow**: this has been presumed to mean some kind of staff or cudgel but the word has not been found elsewhere than in this passage. Corrected copies of the First Quarto read "bat."

270. **foins**: sword thrusts

Glou.   Now let thy friendly hand
Put strength enough to't.   255

                    [*Edgar interposes.*]

Osw.   Wherefore, bold peasant,
Darest thou support a published traitor? Hence!
Lest that th' infection of his fortune take
Like hold on thee. Let go his arm.

Edg. Chill not let go, zir, without vurther 'casion. 260

Osw. Let go, slave, or thou diest!

Edg. Good gentleman, go your gait, and let poor
volk pass. An chud ha' bin zwagger'd out of my life,
'twould not ha' bin zo long as 'tis by a vortnight.
Nay, come not near the old man. Keep out, che vor' 265
ye, or Ise try whither your costard or my ballow be
the harder. Chill be plain with you.

Osw. Out, dunghill!

Edg. Chill pick your teeth, zir. Come! No matter vor
your foins.   270

                    [*They fight and Oswald falls.*]

Osw. Slave, thou hast slain me. Villain, take my purse.
If ever thou wilt thrive, bury my body,
And give the letters which thou find'st about me
To Edmund Earl of Gloucester. Seek him out
Upon the English party. O, untimely death! Death!   275
                                        He dies.

Edg. I know thee well. A serviceable villain,
As duteous to the vices of thy mistress
As badness would desire.

Glou.   What, is he dead?

Edg. Sit you down, father; rest you.   280
Let's see these pockets; the letters that he speaks of
May be my friends. He's dead; I am only sorry
He had no other deathsman. Let us see.

294. **indistinguished space of woman's will:** limitless scope of woman's lust

297. **Thee I'll rake up:** I will bury you (Oswald).

298. **in the mature time:** when the time is ripe

299. **ungracious:** wicked

300. **death-practiced:** whose death is plotted

303. **ingenious:** capable of subtle perception

304. **Better I were:** It would be better if I were

Leave, gentle wax; and manners, blame us not:
To know our enemies' minds, we rip their hearts;   285
Their papers is more lawful.   *Reads the letter.*

*Let our reciprocal vows be remembered. You have
many opportunities to cut him off. If your will want not,
time and place will be fruitfully offered. There is nothing
done if he return the conqueror. Then am I the prisoner,* 290
*and his bed my jail; from the loathed warmth whereof
deliver me, and supply the place for your labor.*

    Your (wife, so I would say) affectionate servant,
                                GONERIL.

O indistinguished space of woman's will!
A plot upon her virtuous husband's life,   295
And the exchange my brother! Here in the sands
Thee I'll rake up, the post unsanctified
Of murderous lechers; and in the mature time
With this ungracious paper strike the sight
Of the death-practiced Duke. For him 'tis well   300
That of thy death and business I can tell.
 Glou. The King is mad. How stiff is my vile sense,
That I stand up, and have ingenious feeling
Of my huge sorrows! Better I were distract.
So should my thoughts be severed from my griefs,   305
And woes by wrong imaginations lose
The knowledge of themselves.
                       A drum afar off.
  Edg.   Give me your hand.
Far off methinks I hear the beaten drum.
Come, father, I'll bestow you with a friend.   *Exeunt.* 310

IV. vii. Cordelia at last has rescued Lear, who is shown sleeping, under the care of a doctor. When he awakes, he is purged of his rage and bitterness and begs Cordelia's forgiveness. The act concludes with news that the enemy is approaching and the end is "like to be bloody."

||||||||||||||||||||||||||||||||||||||

6. **Nor more nor clipped:** neither added to nor abbreviated

11. **Yet to be known shortens my made intent:** to identify myself already would prevent the completion of my purpose.

20. **child-changed:** possibly two meanings are intended: "changed by his children" and "changed to a child."

Scene VII. [A tent in the French camp.]

Enter Cordelia, Kent, Doctor, *and* Gentleman.

Cor. O thou good Kent, how shall I live and work
To match thy goodness? My life will be too short
And every measure fail me.
    Kent. To be acknowledged, madam, is o'erpaid.
All my reports go with the modest truth;   5
Nor more nor clipped, but so.
    Cor.   Be better suited:
These weeds are memories of those worser hours:
I prithee put them off.
    Kent.   Pardon, dear madam.   10
Yet to be known shortens my made intent.
My boon I make it that you know me not
Till time and I think meet.
    Cor. Then be it so, my good lord. [*To the Doctor*] How
      does the King?   15
    Doct. Madam, sleeps still.
    Cor. O you kind gods,
Cure this great breach in his abused nature!
Th' untuned and jarring senses, O, wind up
Of this child-changed father!   20
    Doct.   So please your Majesty
That we may wake the King? He hath slept long.
    Cor. Be governed by your knowledge, and proceed
I' the sway of your own will. Is he arrayed?

Enter Lear *in a chair carried by* Servants.

    Gent. Ay, madam. In the heaviness of sleep   25
We put fresh garments on him.

36. **flakes**: locks of hair

37. **challenged**: demanded

41. **perdu**: a "sentinel perdu" was one stationed in so dangerous a spot that escaping death seemed impossible.

44. **fain**: obliged

48. **concluded all**: both completely ended

57. **wide**: of the mark, wandering in his wits

Doct. Be by, good madam, when we do awake him.
I doubt not of his temperance.
   Cor.   Very well.

                           [*Music.*]

   Doct. Please you draw near. Louder the music there!   30
   Cor. O my dear father, restoration hang
Thy medicine on my lips, and let this kiss
Repair those violent harms that my two sisters
Have in thy reverence made!
   Kent.   Kind and dear princess!   35
   Cor. Had you not been their father, these white flakes
Had challenged pity of them. Was this a face
To be opposed against the warring winds?
To stand against the deep dread-bolted thunder?
In the most terrible and nimble stroke   40
Of quick, cross lightning? to watch—poor perdu!—
With this thin helm? Mine enemy's dog,
Though he had bit me, should have stood that night
Against my fire; and wast thou fain, poor father,
To hovel thee with swine and rogues forlorn,   45
In short and musty straw? Alack, alack!
'Tis wonder that thy life and wits at once
Had not concluded all.—He wakes; speak to him.
   Doct. Madam, do you; 'tis fittest.
   Cor. How does my royal lord? How fares your Majesty?   50
   Lear. You do me wrong to take me out o' the grave.
Thou art a soul in bliss; but I am bound
Upon a wheel of fire, that mine own tears
Do scald like molten lead.
   Cor.   Sir, do you know me?   55
   Lear. You are a spirit, I know. Where did you die?
   Cor. Still, still, far wide!

69. **fond**: doting, i.e., in his dotage

Doct. He's scarce awake. Let him alone awhile.

Lear. Where have I been? Where am I? Fair daylight?
I am mightily abused. I should e'en die with pity,   60
To see another thus. I know not what to say.
I will not swear these are my hands. Let's see:
I feel this pin prick. Would I were assured
Of my condition!

Cor.   O, look upon me, sir,   65
And hold your hands in benediction o'er me.
No, sir, you must not kneel.

Lear.   Pray, do not mock me.
I am a very foolish fond old man,
Fourscore and upward, not an hour more nor less;   70
And, to deal plainly,
I fear I am not in my perfect mind.
Methinks I should know you, and know this man;
Yet I am doubtful; for I am mainly ignorant
What place this is; and all the skill I have   75
Remembers not these garments; nor I know not
Where I did lodge last night. Do not laugh at me;
For (as I am a man) I think this lady
To be my child Cordelia.

Cor.   And so I am, I am.   80

Lear. Be your tears wet? Yes, faith. I pray weep not.
If you have poison for me, I will drink it.
I know you do not love me, for your sisters
Have, as I do remember, done me wrong:
You have some cause, they have not.   85

Cor.   No cause, no cause.

Lear. Am I in France?

Kent.   In your own kingdom, sir.

Lear. Do not abuse me.

92. **even o'er:** fill the gaps in his recollection

94. **settling:** calming, of his mind

107. **arbitrement:** settlement of the dispute

109. **point and period:** synonymous for "final end"; **throughly:** thoroughly

Doct. Be comforted, good madam. The great rage   90
You see is killed in him; and yet it is danger
To make him even o'er the time he has lost.
Desire him to go in. Trouble him no more
Till further settling.

 Cor. Will't please your Highness walk?   95
 Lear.   You must bear with me.
Pray you now, forget and forgive. I am old and foolish.
  Exeunt [*Lear, Cordelia, Doctor, and Attendants*].
 Gent. Holds it true, sir, that the Duke of Cornwall was
so slain?
 Kent. Most certain, sir.   100
 Gent. Who is conductor of his people?
 Kent. As 'tis said, the bastard son of Gloucester.
 Gent. They say Edgar, his banished son, is with the
Earl of Kent in Germany.
 Kent. Report is changeable. 'Tis time to look about;   105
the powers of the kingdom approach apace.
 Gent. The arbitrement is like to be bloody.
Fare you well, sir.   [*Exit.*]
 Kent. My point and period will be throughly wrought,
Or well or ill, as this day's battle's fought.   *Exit.* 110

KING LEAR

ACT V

V. i. Edmund and Regan prepare for battle. When Goneril and Albany appear, Goneril is beside herself with jealousy of her sister. She would rather lose the battle than lose Edmund to Regan. Edgar in disguise gives a letter to Albany which will reveal Edmund's villainy.

‖‖‖‖‖‖‖‖‖‖‖‖‖‖‖‖‖‖‖‖‖‖‖‖‖‖‖‖‖‖‖‖

1, 4. **last purpose, constant pleasure:** final decision
13. **forfended:** prohibited
15-6. **conjunct/ And bosomed with her, as far as we call hers:** as intimate with her as it is possible to be

ACT V

Scene I. [The British camp near Dover.]

Enter, with *Drum* and *Colors, Edmund, Regan, Gentle-men* and *Soldiers.*

Edm. Know of the Duke if his last purpose hold,
Or whether since he is advised by aught
To change the course. He's full of alteration
And self-reproving. Bring his constant pleasure.

[*Exit an Officer.*]

Reg. Our sister's man is certainly miscarried.   5
Edm. 'Tis to be doubted, madam.
Reg.   Now, sweet lord,
You know the goodness I intend upon you.
Tell me, but truly, but then speak the truth,
Do you not love my sister?   10
Edm.   In honored love.
Reg. But have you never found my brother's way
To the forfended place?
Edm.   That thought abuses you.
Reg. I am doubtful that you have been conjunct   15
And bosomed with her, as far as we call hers.
Edm. No, by mine honor, madam.

30-1. **It touches us as France invades our land/ Not bolds the King:** our concern is with the French invasion of our land, not with any assistance France may lend the King. Possibly a corrupt passage; note the repetition of "with others whom," ll. 27 and 31.

34. **Why is this reasoned:** why is reasoning necessary on this matter.

36. **broils:** disputes

39. **ancient of war:** seasoned officers of the force

43. **convenient:** suitable

Reg. I never shall endure her. Dear my lord,
Be not familiar with her.
    Edm.   Fear me not.   20
She and the Duke her husband!

Enter, with *Drum* and *Colors*, Albany, Goneril, Soldiers.

    Gon. [*Aside*] I had rather lose the battle than that
        sister
Should loosen him and me.
    Alb. Our very loving sister, well bemet.   25
Sir, this I hear: the King is come to his daughter,
With others whom the rigor of our state
Forced to cry out. Where I could not be honest,
I never yet was valiant. For this business,
It touches us as France invades our land,   30
Not bolds the King, with others, whom, I fear,
Most just and heavy causes make oppose.
    Edm. Sir, you speak nobly.
    Reg.   Why is this reasoned?
    Gon. Combine together 'gainst the enemy;   35
For these domestic and particular broils
Are not the question here.
    Alb.   Let's then determine
With th' ancient of war on our proceeding.
    Edm. I shall attend you presently at your tent.   40
    Reg. Sister, you'll go with us?
    Gon. No.
    Reg. 'Tis most convenient; pray go with us.
    Gon. [*Aside*] O, ho, I know the riddle.—I will go.

[*As they are going out,*] Enter *Edgar* [*disguised*].

53. **miscarry:** lose the battle and are killed
55. **machination:** plotting (against Albany)
65. **greet the time:** be prepared when the time comes
67. **jealous:** suspiciously watchful

Edg. If e'er your Grace had speech with man so poor,   45
Hear me one word.

    Alb.   I'll overtake you. *Exeunt [all but*
                                      Albany and Edgar].

Speak.

    Edg. Before you fight the battle, ope this letter.
If you have victory, let the trumpet sound   50
For him that brought it. Wretched though I seem,
I can produce a champion that will prove
What is avouched there. If you miscarry,
Your business of the world hath so an end,
And machination ceases. Fortune love you!   55

    Alb. Stay till I have read the letter.

    Edg.   I was forbid it.
When time shall serve, let but the herald cry,
And I'll appear again.

    Alb. Why, fare thee well. I will o'erlook thy paper.   60
                                      Exit [Edgar].

Enter *Edmund.*

    Edm. The enemy's in view; draw up your powers.
Here is the guess of their true strength and forces
By diligent discovery; but your haste
Is now urged on you.

    Alb.   We will greet the time.   *Exit.*   65

    Edm. To both these sisters have I sworn my love;
Each jealous of the other, as the stung
Are of the adder. Which of them shall I take?
Both? one? or neither? Neither can be enjoyed
If both remain alive. To take the widow   70
Exasperates, makes mad her sister Goneril;
And hardly shall I carry out my side,

74. **countenance:** authority

79-80. **my state/ Stands on me to defend, not to debate:** my position can only be maintained by active defense, not by pondering moral issues.

‖‖

V. ii. Cordelia's army crosses the stage on the way to battle. Presently Edgar returns to report that Cordelia's forces have lost and Gloucester, who has been waiting between the two camps, must fly for his life.

‖‖‖‖‖‖‖‖‖‖‖‖‖‖‖‖‖‖‖‖‖‖‖‖‖‖‖‖‖‖‖‖‖

Her husband being alive. Now then, we'll use
His countenance for the battle, which being done,
Let her who would be rid of him devise   75
His speedy taking off. As for the mercy
Which he intends to Lear and to Cordelia,
The battle done, and they within our power,
Shall never see his pardon; for my state
Stands on me to defend, not to debate.   *Exit.*   80

Scene II. [*A field between the two camps.*]

Alarum within. Enter, with *Drum* and *Colors, Lear,
Cordelia,* and the *Powers of France* over the stage, and
exeunt.

Enter *Edgar* and *Gloucester.*

Edg. Here, father, take the shadow of this tree
For your good host. Pray that the right may thrive.
If ever I return to you again,
I'll bring you comfort.
Glou.   Grace go with you, sir!   5
                                        Exit [*Edgar*].

Alarum and retreat within. Enter *Edgar.*

Edg. Away, old man! give me thy hand! away!
King Lear hath lost, he and his daughter ta'en.
Give me thy hand! come on!

V. iii. The final scene opens with Lear and Cordelia prisoners of Edmund, who sends them away under the charge of a captain who has secret instructions to do away with them. Albany appears with Goneril and Regan and takes command from Edmund. Regan and Goneril quarrel over Edmund and Regan dies from poison administered by Goneril, who subsequently stabs herself. Albany proclaims Edmund a traitor and Edgar claims the privilege of combat with him and gives him a mortal wound. Lear comes in bearing Cordelia's body and announces that he had killed the knave who was hanging her. Lear, too, dies. The stage is left to Albany, Kent, and Edgar.

〰〰〰〰〰〰〰〰〰〰

2. **their greater pleasures:** the wishes of those with higher authority

5. **with best meaning:** with the best intentions

17. **take upon's the mystery of things:** undertake to decide the meaning of things

Glou. No further, sir. A man may rot even here.
 Edg. What, in ill thoughts again? Men must endure 10
Their going hence, even as their coming hither;
Ripeness is all. Come on.
 Glou.   And that's true too. *Exeunt.*

Scene III. [The British camp, near Dover.]

*Enter, in conquest, with Drum and Colors, Edmund;
 Lear and Cordelia as prisoners; Soldiers, Captain.*

 Edm. Some officers take them away. Good guard
Until their greater pleasures first be known
That are to censure them.
 Cor.   We are not the first
Who with best meaning have incurred the worst. 5
For thee, oppressed king, I am cast down;
Myself could else outfrown false Fortune's frown.
Shall we not see these daughters and these sisters?
 Lear. No, no, no, no! Come, let's away to prison.
We two alone will sing like birds i' the cage. 10
When thou dost ask me blessing, I'll kneel down
And ask of thee forgiveness. So we'll live,
And pray, and sing, and tell old tales, and laugh
At gilded butterflies, and hear poor rogues
Talk of court news; and we'll talk with them too, 15
Who loses and who wins; who's in, who's out;
And take upon's the mystery of things,
As if we were God's spies; and we'll wear out,

26. **goodyears**: an undefined word of obscure origin connoting a malevolent agency; **fell**: skin

41. **carry it so**: so perform it

In a walled prison, packs and sects of great ones
That ebb and flow by the moon.   20
  Edm.   Take them away.
  Lear. Upon such sacrifices, my Cordelia,
The gods themselves throw incense. Have I caught thee?
He that parts us shall bring a brand from heaven
And fire us hence like foxes. Wipe thine eyes.   25
The goodyears shall devour 'em, flesh and fell,
Ere they shall make us weep! We'll see 'em starved first.
Come.   *Exeunt* [*Lear and Cordelia, guarded*].
  Edm.   Come hither, Captain; hark.
Take thou this note [*gives a paper*]. Go follow them to   30
    prison.
One step I have advanced thee; if thou dost
As this instructs thee, thou dost make thy way
To noble fortunes. Know thou this, that men
Are as the time is; to be tender-minded   35
Does not become a sword. Thy great employment
Will not bear question; either say thou'lt do't,
Or thrive by other means.
  Capt.   I'll do't, my lord.
  Edm. About it! and write happy when th' hast done. 40
Mark—I say, instantly; and carry it so
As I have set it down.
  Capt. I cannot draw a cart, nor eat dried oats;
If it be man's work, I'll do't.   *Exit.*

  Flourish. Enter *Albany, Goneril, Regan, Soldiers.*

  Alb. Sir, you have showed today your valiant strain, 45
And fortune led you well. You have the captives
Who were the opposites of this day's strife;

56. **impressed lances:** weapons of recruited soldiers

67. **hold you:** regard you

69. **list:** please

73. **immediacy:** immediate representation of myself

79. **compeers:** equals

I do require them of you, so to use them
As we shall find their merits and our safety
May equally determine. 50
    Edm. Sir, I thought it fit
To send the old and miserable King
To some retention and appointed guard;
Whose age had charms in it, whose title more,
To pluck the common bosom on his side 55
And turn our impressed lances in our eyes
Which do command them. With him I sent the Queen,
My reason all the same; and they are ready
Tomorrow, or at further space, t' appear
Where you shall hold your session. At this time 60
We sweat and bleed: the friend hath lost his friend,
And the best quarrels, in the heat, are cursed
By those that feel their sharpness.
The question of Cordelia and her father
Requires a fitter place. 65
    Alb. Sir, by your patience,
I hold you but a subject of this war,
Not as a brother.
    Reg. That's as we list to grace him.
Methinks our pleasure might have been demanded 70
Ere you had spoke so far. He led our powers,
Bore the commission of my place and person,
The which immediacy may well stand up
And call itself your brother.
    Gon. Not so hot! 75
In his own grace he doth exalt himself
More than in your addition.
    Reg. In my rights
By me invested, he compeers the best.
    Gon. That were the most if he should husband you. 80

85. **From a full-flowing stomach:** with a stream of angry words. "Stomach" was often used to mean anger.

87. **the walls are thine:** that is, I surrender the fortress of my person to you.

88. **Witness the world:** let the world witness

91. **The let-alone lies not in your good will:** you have no power of prevention.

93. **Half-blooded:** illegitimate

97. **in thine attaint:** as a partner of your treason

102. **banes:** banns

105. **An interlude:** ironically, "a pretty farce"

110. **make:** make good

Reg. Jesters do oft prove prophets.

Gon.   Holla, holla!
That eye that told you so looked but asquint.

Reg. Lady, I am not well; else I should answer
From a full-flowing stomach. General,   85
Take thou my soldiers, prisoners, patrimony;
Dispose of them, of me; the walls are thine.
Witness the world that I create thee here
My lord and master.

Gon.   Mean you to enjoy him?   90

Alb. The let-alone lies not in your good will.

Edm. Nor in thine, lord.

Alb.   Half-blooded fellow, yes.

Reg. [*To Edmund*] Let the drum strike, and prove my
     title thine.   95

Alb. Stay yet; hear reason. Edmund, I arrest thee
On capital treason; and, in thine attaint,
This gilded serpent [*points to Goneril*]. For your claim,
     fair sister,
I bar it in the interest of my wife.   100
'Tis she is sub-contracted to this lord,
And I, her husband, contradict your banes.
If you will marry, make your loves to me;
My lady is bespoke.

Gon.   An interlude!   105

Alb. Thou art armed, Gloucester. Let the trumpet
     sound.
If none appear to prove upon thy person
Thy heinous, manifest, and many treasons,
There is my pledge [*throws down a glove*]! I'll make it on 110
     thy heart,
Ere I taste bread, thou art in nothing less
Than I have here proclaimed thee.

120. **maintain**: defend
124. **virtue**: valor

 Reg.   Sick, O, sick!
 Gon. [*Aside*] If not, I'll ne'er trust medicine. 115
 Edm. There's my exchange [*throws down a glove*].
  What in the world he is
That names me traitor, villain-like he lies.
Call by thy trumpet. He that dares approach,
On him, on you, who not? I will maintain 120
My truth and honor firmly.
 Alb. A herald, ho!
 Edm.   A herald, ho, a herald!
 Alb. Trust to thy single virtue; for thy soldiers,
All levied in my name, have in my name 125
Took their discharge.
 Reg.   My sickness grows upon me.
 Alb. She is not well. Convey her to my tent.
         [*Exit Regan, led.*]

Enter a *Herald.*

Come hither, herald. Let the trumpet sound,
And read out this. 130
 Capt. Sound, trumpet! *A trumpet sounds.*

 Her. (*Reads*) *If any man of quality or degree within
the lists of the army will maintain upon Edmund, supposed Earl of Gloucester, that he is a manifold traitor, let
him appear by the third sound of the trumpet. He is bold* 135
in his defense. *First trumpet.*

 Her. Again! *Second trumpet.*
 Her. Again! *Third trumpet.*
      Trumpet answers within.

146. **canker-bit:** eaten as by caterpillars, from within, an allusion to Edmund's treacherous undermining of his reputation

148. **cope:** meet in combat

158. **Maugre:** despite

166. **bent:** directed

Enter *Edgar*, armed, a *Trumpet* before him.

Alb. Ask him his purposes, why he appears   140
Upon this call o' the trumpet.
    Her.   What are you?
Your name, your quality? and why you answer
This present summons?
    Edg.   Know my name is lost;   145
By treason's tooth bare-gnawn and canker-bit.
Yet am I noble as the adversary
I come to cope.
    Alb.   Which is that adversary?
    Edg. What's he that speaks for Edmund Earl of   150
    Gloucester?
    Edm. Himself. What sayest thou to him?
    Edg.   Draw thy sword,
That, if my speech offend a noble heart,
Thy arm may do thee justice. Here is mine.   155
Behold, it is the privilege of mine honors,
My oath, and my profession. I protest,
Maugre thy strength, place, youth, and eminence,
Despite thy victor sword and fire-new fortune,
Thy valor and thy heart, thou art a traitor,   160
False to thy gods, thy brother, and thy father;
Conspirant 'gainst this high illustrious prince;
And from th' extremest upward of thy head
To the descent and dust beneath thy foot,
A most toad-spotted traitor. Say thou "no,"   165
This sword, this arm, and my best spirits are bent
To prove upon thy heart, whereto I speak,
Thou liest.
    Edm.   In wisdom I should ask thy name;

171. **say:** smack

172. **safe and nicely:** cautiously and with close attention to interpreting the rules

177-78. **This sword of mine shall give them instant way/ Where they shall rest for ever:** "them" and "they" refer to the charges of treason. My sword will toss the charges of treason back to rest on your head.

180. **practice:** trickery; see I. ii. 176.

But since thy outside looks so fair and warlike,   170
And that thy tongue some say of breeding breathes,
What safe and nicely I might well delay
By rule of knighthood, I disdain and spurn;
Back do I toss those treasons to thy head,
With the hell-hated lie o'erwhelm thy heart,   175
Which, for they yet glance by and scarcely bruise,
This sword of mine shall give them instant way
Where they shall rest for ever. Trumpets, speak!
                    Alarums. Fight. [Edmund falls.]
    Alb. Save him, save him!
    Gon.   This is mere practice, Gloucester.   180
By the law of arms thou wast not bound to answer
An unknown opposite. Thou art not vanquished,
But cozened and beguiled.
    Alb.   Shut your mouth, dame,
Or with this paper shall I stop it. [*Shows her her letter to*   185
    Edmund.]—[*To Edmund*] Hold, sir.
[*To Goneril*] Thou worse than any name, read thine own
    evil.
No tearing, lady! I perceive you know it.
    Gon. Say if I do—the laws are mine, not thine.   190
Who can arraign me for't?
    Alb.   Most monstrous! O!
Knowest thou this paper?
    Gon.   Ask me not what I know.   *Exit.*
    Alb. Go after her. She's desperate; govern her.   195
                    [*Exit an Officer.*]
    Edm. What you have charged me with, that have I
    done,
And more, much more. The time will bring it out.
'Tis past, and so am I. But what art thou

Of the mutabylyte of fortune

That man whiche hopyth hye vp to ascende
On fortunes whele, and come to state royall
If the whele turne, may doute sore to descende
If he be hye the sorer is his fall
So he whiche trustyth nat therto at all
Shall in moste ese and suerty hymselfe gyde
For vnsure fortune can in no place abyde

Fortune's wheel.
From Sebastian Brant's *Ship of Fools* (1497)

202. Let's exchange charity: I will forgive you your crimes as you forgive my killing you.

203. I am no less in blood than thou art: my blood is as good as yours.

211. The wheel: Fortune's wheel

That hast this fortune on me? If thou'rt noble,   200
I do forgive thee.
   Edg.   Let's exchange charity.
I am no less in blood than thou art, Edmund;
If more, the more th' hast wronged me.
My name is Edgar and thy father's son.   205
The gods are just, and of our pleasant vices
Make instruments to plague us.
The dark and vicious place where thee he got
Cost him his eyes.
   Edm.   Th' hast spoken right; 'tis true.   210
The wheel is come full circle; I am here.
   Alb. Methought thy very gait did prophesy
A royal nobleness. I must embrace thee.
Let sorrow split my heart if ever I
Did hate thee, or thy father!   215
   Edg.   Worthy prince, I know't.
   Alb. Where have you hid yourself?
How have you known the miseries of your father?
   Edg. By nursing them, my lord. List a brief tale;
And when 'tis told, O that my heart would burst!   220
The bloody proclamation to escape
That followed me so near (O, our lives' sweetness!
That we the pain of death would hourly die
Rather than die at once!) taught me to shift
Into a madman's rags, t' assume a semblance   225
That very dogs disdained; and in this habit
Met I my father with his bleeding rings,
Their precious stones new lost; became his guide,
Led him, begged for him, saved him from despair;
Never (O fault!) revealed myself unto him   230
Until some half hour past, when I was armed;

248. **big**: loud
256. **puissant**: powerful

Not sure, though hoping of this good success,
I asked his blessing, and from first to last
Told him my pilgrimage. But his flawed heart
(Alack, too weak the conflict to support!)   235
'Twixt two extremes of passion, joy and grief,
Burst smilingly.
    Edm.   This speech of yours hath moved me,
And shall perchance do good; but speak you on;
You look as you had something more to say.   240
    Alb. If there be more, more woeful, hold it in;
For I am almost ready to dissolve,
Hearing of this.
    Edg.   This would have seemed a period
To such as love not sorrow; but another,   245
To amplify too much, would make much more,
And top extremity.
Whilst I was big in clamor, came there a man,
Who, having seen me in my worst estate,
Shunned my abhorred society; but then, finding   250
Who 'twas that so endured, with his strong arms
He fastened on my neck, and bellowed out
As he'd burst heaven; threw him on my father;
Told the most piteous tale of Lear and him
That ever ear received; which in recounting   255
His grief grew puissant, and the strings of life
Began to crack. Twice then the trumpets sounded,
And there I left him tranced.
    Alb.   But who was this?
    Edg. Kent, sir, the banished Kent; who in disguise   260
Followed his enemy king and did him service
Improper for a slave.

279. very: mere

Enter a *Gentleman* with a bloody knife.

Gent. Help, help! O, help!

Edg.   What kind of help?

Alb.   Speak, man.   265

Edg. What means this bloody knife?

Gent.   'Tis hot, it smokes.

It came even from the heart of—O, she's dead!

Alb. Who dead? Speak, man.

Gent. Your lady, sir, your lady! and her sister   270

By her is poisoned; she hath confessed it.

Edm. I was contracted to them both. All three

Now marry in an instant.

Edg.   Here comes Kent.

Enter *Kent*.

Alb. Produce the bodies, be they alive or dead.   275

                  [Exit Gentleman.]

This judgment of the heavens, that makes us tremble,

Touches us not with pity. *[To Kent]* O, is this he?

The time will not allow the compliment

Which very manners urges.

Kent.   I am come   280

To bid my king and master aye good night.

Is he not here?

Alb.   Great thing of us forgot!

Speak, Edmund, where's the King? and where's Cordelia?

      The bodies of Goneril and Regan are brought in.

Seest thou this object, Kent?   285

Kent. Alack, why thus?

305. **fordid:** killed
312. **stone:** crystal surface of a mirror

Edm.   Yet Edmund was beloved.
The one the other poisoned for my sake,
And after slew herself.
    Alb. Even so. Cover their faces.   290
    Edm. I pant for life. Some good I mean to do,
Despite of mine own nature. Quickly send
(Be brief in't) to the castle; for my writ
Is on the life of Lear and on Cordelia.
Nay, send in time.   295
    Alb.   Run, run, O, run!
    Edg. To who, my lord? Who has the office? Send
Thy token of reprieve.
    Edm. Well thought on. Take my sword;
Give it the Captain.   300
    Edg.   Haste thee for thy life. [*Exit an Officer.*]
    Edm. He hath commission from thy wife and me
To hang Cordelia in the prison and
To lay the blame upon her own despair
That she fordid herself.   305
    Alb. The gods defend her! Bear him hence awhile.
                   [*Edmund is borne off.*]

Enter *Lear*, with *Cordelia* in his arms, [*Captain* and
              others following*].

    Lear. Howl, howl, howl! O, you are men of stones.
Had I your tongues and eyes, I'd use them so
That heaven's vault should crack. She's gone for ever!
I know when one is dead, and when one lives.   310
She's dead as earth. Lend me a looking glass.
If that her breath will mist or stain the stone,
Why, then she lives.
    Kent.   Is this the promised end?

316. **Fall and cease:** addressed to the heavens
331. **falchion:** a sword
333. **crosses:** troubles
344. **difference and decay:** decline of fortune

Edg. Or image of that horror? 315

Alb. Fall and cease!

Lear. This feather stirs; she lives! If it be so,
It is a chance which does redeem all sorrows
That ever I have felt.

Kent. O my good master! 320

Lear. Prithee away!

Edg. 'Tis noble Kent, your friend.

Lear. A plague upon you, murderers, traitors all!
I might have saved her; now she's gone for ever!
Cordelia, Cordelia! stay a little. Ha! 325
What is't thou sayest? Her voice was ever soft,
Gentle, and low—an excellent thing in woman.
I killed the slave that was a-hanging thee.

Capt. 'Tis true, my lords, he did.

Lear. Did I not, fellow? 330
I have seen the day, with my good biting falchion
I would have made 'em skip. I am old now,
And these same crosses spoil me. Who are you?
Mine eyes are not o' the best, I'll tell you straight.

Kent. If fortune brag of two she loved and hated, 335
One of them we behold.

Lear. This is a dull sight. Are you not Kent?

Kent. The same;
Your servant Kent. Where is your servant Caius?

Lear. He's a good fellow, I can tell you that. 340
He'll strike, and quickly too. He's dead and rotten.

Kent. No, my good lord; I am the very man—

Lear. I'll see that straight.

Kent. That from your first of difference and decay
Have followed your sad steps. 345

Lear. You are welcome hither.

347. **Nor no man else:** not I nor anyone. Kent
means that this is no time for formal greetings.

354. **bootless:** unprofitable

358. **this great decay:** this ruined man, Lear

367. **fool:** a term of endearment, referring to Cordelia

Kent. Nor no man else! All's cheerless, dark, and
   deadly.
Your eldest daughters have fordone themselves,
And desperately are dead.   350
   Lear.   Ay, so I think.
   Alb. He knows not what he says; and vain is it
That we present us to him.
   Edg.   Very bootless.

Enter a *Captain.*

   Capt. Edmund is dead, my lord.   355
   Alb.   That's but a trifle here.
You lords and noble friends, know our intent.
What comfort to this great decay may come
Shall be applied. For us, we will resign,
During the life of this old Majesty,   360
To him our absolute power; [*to Edgar and Kent*] you to
   your rights;
With boot, and such addition as your honors
Have more than merited. All friends shall taste
The wages of their virtue, and all foes   365
The cup of their deservings.—O, see, see!
   Lear. And my poor fool is hanged! No, no, no life!
Why should a dog, a horse, a rat, have life,
And thou no breath at all? Thou'lt come no more,
Never, never, never, never, never!   370
Pray you undo this button. Thank you, sir.
Do you see this? Look on her! look! her lips!
Look there, look there!   *He dies.*
   Edg.   He faints! My lord, my lord!
   Kent. Break, heart; I prithee break!   375
   Edg.   Look up, my lord.

382. **usurped his life**: lived beyond the natural limits of his life

386. **gored**: wounded

    Kent. Vex not his ghost. O, let him pass! He hates him
That would upon the rack of this tough world
Stretch him out longer.
    Edg.   He is gone indeed.   380
    Kent. The wonder is, he hath endured so long.
He but usurped his life.
    Alb. Bear them from hence. Our present business
Is general woe. [*To Kent and Edgar*] Friends of my soul,
    you twain   385
Rule in this realm, and the gored state sustain.
    Kent. I have a journey, sir, shortly to go.
My master calls me; I must not say no.
    Edg. The weight of this sad time we must obey,
Speak what we feel, not what we ought to say.   390
The oldest hath borne most; we that are young
Shall never see so much, nor live so long.

                    Exeunt with a dead march.

The Folger Library

GENERAL READER'S EDITIONS

Edited by Louis B. Wright, Director,
and Virginia A. LaMar, Executive Secretary, The Folger Shakespeare Library

PUBLISHED BY WASHINGTON SQUARE PRESS, INC.

AVAILABLE IN THIS SERIES:

Titles in this distinguished series will be in
creased to 45¢ retail when new printings are made.